Jimmy Little
A Yorta Yorta Man

Jimmy Little
A Yorta Yorta Man

Frances Peters-Little

Hardie Grant
BOOKS

Published in 2023 by Hardie Grant Books, an imprint of Hardie Grant Publishing

Hardie Grant Books (Melbourne)
Wurundjeri Country
Building 1, 658 Church Street
Richmond, Victoria 3121

Hardie Grant Books (London)
5th & 6th Floors
52–54 Southwark Street
London SE1 1UN

hardiegrant.com/au/books

All rights reserved. No part of this publication may be reproduced, stored in a retrieval system or transmitted in any form by any means, electronic, mechanical, photocopying, recording or otherwise, without the prior written permission of the publishers and copyright holders.

The moral rights of the authors have been asserted.

Copyright text © Frances Peters-Little 2023

'Kumanjay Little' lyrics © Ti Tree Kids, Seraphina Presley-Haines, Seini Taumoepeau & Mal Webb 2012

A list of image credits and copyright acknowledgements is listed on page 245.

Every effort has been made to trace copyright holders and to obtain their permission for the use of copyright material. Please contact the publisher with any information on errors or omissions.

 A catalogue record for this book is available from the National Library of Australia

Jimmy Little: A Yorta Yorta Man
ISBN 978 1 74379 906 2

10 9 8 7 6 5 4 3 2 1

Publisher: Pam Brewster
Cover design: Celia Mance
Cover photography by John Elliott (front), Pierre Baroni (back)
Internal design: Nada Backovic
Typeset in Adobe Jenson Pro by Kirby Jones
Printed in Australia by Griffin Press, part of Ovato, an Accredited ISO AS/NZS 14001 Environmental Management System printer.

 The paper this book is printed on is certified against the Forest Stewardship Council® Standards. Griffin Press holds chain of custody certification SCS-COC-001185. FSC® promotes environmentally responsible, socially beneficial and economically viable management of the world's forests.

Hardie Grant acknowledges the Traditional Owners of the country on which we work, the Wurundjeri people of the Kulin nation and the Gadigal people of the Eora nation, and recognises their continuing connection to the land, waters and culture. We pay our respects to their Elders past and present.

*This book is dedicated to my son,
James Henry Little.*

Foreword

Deborah Cheetham AO

My uncle held the status of legend in so many Australian homes, and mine was no exception.

I first met my uncle when he was performing at a local suburban shopping centre – which in the early 1970s was still a relatively new phenomenon. My adopted mother had gone to particular lengths that morning to make sure I was looking my best and ready to make the trip to Miranda Fair shopping centre. I was barely six years old but I recall feeling somewhat overdressed for the occasion in my scratchy Sunday clothes, my feet crammed into patent leather shoes.

My insistent questioning of this choice of outfit was met by my adopted mother patiently explaining to me that I was going to meet my Uncle Jimmy and she wanted me to look my best. 'Who is Uncle Jimmy?' I asked absent-mindedly, tugging at the lace trimmed ankle socks, which were not at all symmetrical and were beginning to bother me greatly. 'You will see,' replied my mother in an uncharacteristically enigmatic fashion.

As we arrived at our destination, I could hear music rising above the customary hum of the shopping mall. I was instantly entranced, drawn to it.

Telephone to glory, oh, what joy divine.

Hundreds of people were gathered, entranced just as I was in that moment. The velvety smooth voice of the man singing on stage was matched by his elegant appearance. His warm, generous smile was captivating.

'That's your Uncle Jimmy,' whispered my mother.

Could it be true? The man who was performing on stage, holding everyone in a trance, was my uncle? In my world any adult friend of my parents was introduced as 'Uncle this' or 'Aunty that' so it did not instantly dawn on me that we were actually related.

After the performance ended, we made our way backstage. I remember precious little of the moments I shared with Uncle Jimmy on that occasion, except that it was definitely the first time I had ever seen anyone who looked like me. He was then, and for some years later, the only Aboriginal man I had ever met.

He was famous. He was adored by music loving fans, and he was my uncle.

As my mother and I left the backstage area, I tried to make sense of what had just occurred but given I was only six years old I was a long way from understanding.

'Can we come back and see Uncle Jimmy again tomorrow?' I asked optimistically. My mother did not answer but I could see in her eyes that the answer was no.

It would be the best part of three decades before I would fully appreciate my status as a member of the Stolen Generations and what havoc that punishing reality had wrecked upon my Aboriginal mother Monica, and the wave of grief felt on her behalf by her sister Betty and her brothers Colin, Freddy and in particular, her eldest brother Jimmy. As a young child I had no real concept of my Aboriginal belonging. But upon meeting Uncle Jimmy I felt an instant bond as I saw him perform live and witnessed the power of his music.

Years later, after being reunited with Monica, I came to fully understand the strength of music in the Little family. It was our way of knowing and being. I belonged to a musical family.

*

In 2007, after a twenty year career in classical music, I began a project designed to address the underrepresentation of Indigenous Australians in the world of classical vocal music. I decided to write an opera that would demand an Indigenous cast. I worked on the principal that if I built it, they would come. The opera was called *Pecan Summer* and told the story of the walk-off from Cummeragunja Mission in 1939. This was a moment in history when the women and the men of Yorta Yorta Nation took their destiny into their own hands and walked off the mission in protest of the appalling conditions that had been imposed on them.

I chose this story for its obvious dramatic content; the exodus of Yorta Yorta people from their homeland and the inevitable and unending search for belonging are stories of an epic scale that are both perfectly suited to and deserving of an opera.

Less than a month into researching the history of the walk-off I made a remarkable discovery. The Aboriginal grandparents I had never known – James 'Kunkus' and Sissy Little – were part of the story I was telling. They had carried their firstborn son, my Uncle Jimmy, off the Mission, crossing the Dhungala from New South Wales into Victoria. Suddenly I had a family that stretched beyond the limits of my knowledge. And people were telling me how much I reminded them of my grandmother Sissy, how she had been a singer with a beautiful voice known to one and all.

Suddenly I had a past that linked up with my present and my future, and I just happened to be writing an opera about it. Sadly, Monica and Sissy did not live to see *Pecan Summer* when it finally came to life, but their stories are threaded through each page of the libretto, and their voices can be heard in every note of the score.

It was during the development period for *Pecan Summer* that I spent time with my cousin, and the author of this biography, Frances Peters-Little. We had been working together in Canberra on a film and after my recording session Frances drove me back to the airport. We were just in sight of the Canberra terminal when Frances pulled off the road. 'There is something I have to tell you.'

Frances explained that when I was six years old, Uncle Jimmy had enlisted the help of Charlie Perkins to convince my adoptive parents that he and his wife, Aunty Marjorie, could provide a home for me where I would grow up with family and community.

They came to my parents' home in the southern suburbs of Sydney and pleaded their case on the front doorstep. My adopted mother, Marjory Cheetham, had no intention of inviting two Aboriginal men into our home and nothing could convince her that I belonged anywhere else. Frances' voice trembled as she recounted the story from her point of view. So confident was Jimmy that he could ultimately convince my parents to give me back to my

Aboriginal family that he had told Frances that she would soon have a little sister.

I was stunned by this new revelation, this sliding doors moment. What could have been? A life in music most certainly, perhaps not opera, but who is to say? My Uncle Jimmy wanted to be a father to me. He had pleaded with my adopted mother on that day in 1971. But the answer was no. Upon hearing this from Frances, my mind flew instantly back to the day I found myself in my Sunday clothes – heading across the Georges River towards Miranda Fair for my one and only childhood encounter with the man who in traditional society would have been a father to me.

I have tried, in my life and my career, to be as much like this kind and loving man as I possibly can be. Dr Jimmy Little AO: Poet, philosopher, husband, father, grandfather, and my uncle.

December 2022

Contents

Preface: A Long and Difficult Journey	1
1. 'Yorta Yorta Man'	7
2. 'Homeland'	17
3. 'Woorigee'	35
4. 'Round the Campfires of Old Wallaga Lake'	49
5. 'Life is like a Lottery'	63
6. 'Waterloo Town Hall'	81
7. 'A Choice of Three'	95
8. 'Royal Telephone'	109
9. 'Money Matters'	125
10. 'Who's to Say'	139
11. 'Four Seasons of Life'	155
12. 'Reincarnation'	173
13. 'Guided by His Love'	187
Notes	211
Appendix	223
Credits	245
Acknowledgements	247
Index	249

Aboriginal and Torres Strait Islander readers are advised that this book contains the names and images of people who have died.

PREFACE

A Long and Difficult Journey

It was a strange, long turn of events that brought me to writing the biography of my father. I had been living in Canberra, writing my master's thesis at the Australian National University, which I finally submitted in 2002. My parents and I were sitting in a motel room waiting for Dad to get ready for a performance at Tilley's Devine Cafe Gallery in Lyneham. Dad was shaving and my mother was sitting on the bed when she told me that my father's manager, Buzz Bidstrup, had approached him about having his biography written. It seemed to be the way to go, following on from his recent success with producer Brendan Gallagher with the *Messenger* album.

My parents had decided that I should write the book. I replied that I was not up to the task, that I did not have the time to commit to such an undertaking, but that I would help them find the best possible person to do it. I also panicked, thinking that I might disappoint them, particularly since I thought they had too high an opinion of my abilities. Looking back on that now, I do wonder if I should have stuck with my initial instincts, but my parents told me that no one could write the story better than me; I knew more about his life and was therefore the most qualified person to do the job. So, after years of their insistence, I agreed.

Initially I thought it might work to base my PhD thesis on my dad's life, but despite constant support and encouragement from my supervisors – Professors Ann Curthoys and Peter Read, whom I cannot possibly thank enough for their help and patience – it became evident that I simply could not write this as an academic text. Dad's biography needed to be subjective, and not overembellished with historical detail. So, with that, I began the work.

Over the years, though, I have struggled with making the transition from academic writing to a more personal account and this made the journey a long and difficult one.

If that had not been complicated enough for me, Dad's death in 2012 meant it became even more difficult for me. If it appears that, on occasion, I have slipped into academic discourse in this work, I apologise in advance. I would be happy to leave any criticisms to those who think I have not served his story adequately. The same can be said for those who have been writing about my dad's career over the decades; I hope I have managed to avoid repeating them. The best I can hope for this book is that it provides an opportunity for others to learn more about my father, Jimmy Little, from his daughter's perspective.

Although there have been literally hundreds of articles, news items, sound recordings, interviews and video recordings, there has yet to be a book that was exclusively written about Jimmy Little the person. I am aware of the following written works: the entry in the *Australian Dictionary of Biography* (2021); *Remembering Aboriginal Heroes: Struggle, Identity and the Media* by John Ramsland and Christopher Mooney (2012); *Deadly Sounds,*

Deadly Places: Contemporary Aboriginal Music in Australia by Peter Dunbar-Hill and Chris Gibson (2004); Clinton Walker's *Buried Country: The Story of Aboriginal Country Music* (2000); and the *Oxford Companion to Aboriginal Arts and Culture* (2000), edited by Sylvia Kleinert, Margo Neale et. al. In terms of documentary films, I have relied upon interviews with my father in the 60-minute film titled *Jimmy Little's Gentle Journey* (2003) by Sean Kennedy; the *Australian Biography, Series 6* by Film Australia (1998); the DVD of the Jimmy Little Memorial Concert at the Sydney Opera House (2012); and his own television series called *Little Bit Deadly*, which aired on NITV (2005).

In the print media, numerous articles have been written about him, from *Dawn Magazine* (1954) to his obituary in several national newspapers and television items (2012). As far as radio interviews with him go, there are so many that the task of transcribing them would have been exhausting, so unfortunately some details may be lost forever. In writing this book, I have mostly relied on an interview I did with my father Jimmy in 2003. All paragraphs appearing as sans serif blocks of text are my father's own words from this interview. Parts of this interview are quoted in each of the chapters, and the last two chapters also rely heavily on email correspondence with Brendan Gallagher and Graham 'Buzz' Bidstrup, and were edited by Carole Lander.

The misconceptions

Perhaps one of the most popular views about Jimmy Little's rise to fame is that Australia was ready for an Aboriginal pop star: that the policies of the day, along with social tolerance being at a high, made it easier for people to accept him into the mainstream. This view, however, is fraught with the expectations of those who only thought in political terms and not in artistic terms. They are forgetting that White audiences were already attracted to Black singers from across the globe, an attraction that extended from the 1920s in the United States of America through to the 1960s in the United Kingdom. It is hardly true to say the world was 'tolerant' towards Black singers, because it was not; rather, their musical styles, from Blues to Jazz to Rock and Roll, were intoxicating and were thus embraced by many, even in the times of public lynching, segregation and apartheid. In these ruthless times, it was of course harder for Black singers to gain the same respect as White ones in the mainstream radio and recording industries. In the print media, it was not unusual for my parents to be referred to as 'darkies' who came from 'humpies' (makeshift shelters), and I was referred to as a piccaninny (an offensive term used to refer to Aboriginal children). Despite this sort of thinking, White audiences could not get enough of Black singers.

The other belief that Australians were more tolerant of Aboriginal people during the 1950s is also untrue. There was barely any publicity about the political campaigns of Aboriginal people during the 1950s, nobody was singing songs on the radio in Aboriginal languages or about treaties and stolen children. Even the 1967 Referendum and the Australian civil rights movements only happened *after* Jimmy Little became a radio star and national pop idol. Also, the broader Australian population were not widely aware of the assimilation programs of the 1950s, so the argument that Jimmy Little gained popularity because Australian people cared about Aboriginal issues and people is not only incorrect, but also demeaning in the sense that his talent mattered less to his audiences than his Aboriginality. And, as this book will reveal, there were others who thought his popularity spread across mainstream Australia because he 'sat on the fence' over issues pertaining to Aboriginal rights, and that he did little to advance the cause, which is also untrue.

Another misconception is that he only sang country and western. In this book I intend to demonstrate that his musical styles were highly versatile, to say the least, although it was his country and western fans who kept his career buoyant. Jimmy Little was able to break into all genres of music and gain popularity among the different classes, generations and cultures, which is something few singers can do. Perhaps the only observation I do take onboard is that Jimmy's hit with 'Royal Telephone' struck a chord with Australian audiences because Australians of that era were predominantly Christian, but even then, not all Christians approved of the song, because it was adapted from a Lutheran hymn, and there was deep division among Christians of that era. But this book does address this, and Jimmy was indeed a Christian; his ideas about Christianity, though, were unorthodox. He was, after all, a Yorta Yorta man.

CHAPTER 1

'Yorta Yorta Man'

I was born on the banks of the Murray
Yorta Yorta is my mother's tribal stand
I'm her son, but my father's name I carry
As I walk though this great and ancient land
My father taught me all the things I needed
Like identity and dignity with love
From his southern tribal coastal ways of living
Wallaga Lake and Guluga Mountain high above

I'm a Koori and I come from Cummeragunja
Where my people and my Dreaming all began
Someday I know that I will be returning
Like the legend of my tribal boomerang
My tribal ways are strong and not forgotten
Though my city ways of living, well they may be grand
But I could pack it up yeah and leave it all tomorrow
And go back to my Yorta Yorta clan

> *The nature of the bush and all its beauty*
> *Gives me strength in my will to understand*
> *That no matter where I go, my river people*
> *Will be waiting for this Yorta Yorta Man*
> *I'm a Koori and I come from Cummeragunja*
> *Where my people and my Dreaming all began*
> *Someday I know that I will be returning*
> *Like the legend of my tribal boomerang*[1]

Jimmy wrote his autobiographical song 'Yorta Yorta Man' at a time when he felt that, on a personal level, it was right for him to do so. Having grown up surrounded by so many famous Yorta Yorta people like William Cooper, he also knew there were so many ways of being a strong Yorta Yorta man, and, for Jimmy, that meant choosing to be a singer like his parents. He says he initially wrote the song as a way of answering the questions people asked him – mind you, one of the first things Aboriginal people ask each other is 'where are you from' – and most certainly the song was a defining statement that he was a Koori and proud of where he came from, and that someday his spirit would return to his Dreaming.

Perhaps it's not that obvious to some people that I'm singing about my spirit returning to Cummeragunja, leaving the place of my birth, going out into the world and, at the end of my lifespan, that my spirit would return to the land of my mother's people and there I would rest in my spirit. But there's so many places, like my dad's place at Wallaga Lake, that are equally home to me, and the place where my wife came from in Walgett. So, as I've grown and lived through life, I've wondered where my spirit will finally go to rest. Initially the song came from people asking me questions about where I came from, what state, what part of the state and what my family background was like. So I thought, well, if I wrote a song about it, then perhaps they'd stop asking. So that's what prompted me to write the song. Then I realised I was doing more than writing a song; I was making a statement that I'm very proud of.[2]

Music had always been part of Jimmy Little's life. It was his greatest love and influence. He also loved words, films, football, the bush and philosophising with people. He did not do small talk. In his own words, he was not a political activist, nor a leader, and he never claimed to be a cultural Elder, but, in spite of himself, he became all three. He was, however, raised with Christian values, to which he adapted his Aboriginal beliefs, and he loved country music, although he could sing anything. He was his mother and his father's son first and foremost, believing in the tender and simple gifts they passed on to him. Growing up in a time when Aboriginal people were denied so many of the basic human freedoms most Australians took for granted, Jimmy walked his own path through life as a gentle, softly spoken Aboriginal man from the old school.

His father, Jimmy Edward 'Kunkus' Little senior, was a vaudevillian during the 1930s. Kunkus had been a member of the Wallaga Lake Gum Leaf Band, which was a group of musicians who made music by playing gumleaves – they would place a gumleaf between their lips and blow, which made high pitch sounds. Kunkus remarkably walked 670 kilometres from Wallaga Lake to Melbourne just to perform, then headed back up north to meet with the local Aboriginal choir and vaudevillians at Cummeragunja – an Aboriginal mission 250 kilometres north of Melbourne, along the Murray river on the New South Wales border. The journey from Wallaga may have taken them about a year to complete, with the band performing at various locations, camping out under the stars at night, and mostly living off whatever food they caught and cooked along the way. After purchasing their Ford truck in Melbourne, the band's intention was to meet with the Cummeragunja Choir and tour the Riverina and Goulburn Valley together.[3]

Jimmy's mother, Frances 'Sissy' McGee.

When it came time for the band to leave Cummeragunja, though, some of the choir girls weren't keen for them to go, and rumour has it that they filled the truck's petrol tank with sugar to prevent the men from driving off, in the hope they would stay a little longer.[4] The choir girls' plan worked. What the Gum Leaf lads may have expected would be a short sojourn turned out to be an extended stay of several years.[5] And this is where Kunkus met and married his bride, Frances 'Sissy' McGee, who sang with the choir.

I don't remember my mother playing an instrument or anything like that, but she sang and she yodelled. It was commonplace in those days for males and females to whistle and yodel, and it was reported by people through the ages that Mum had a beautiful voice. Swiss yodelling, at that time, was considered to be very special and whoever had the ability to do it was thought of pretty highly.

The Cummeragunja Choir was considered to be impressive whenever they held their concerts in the Cummeragunja dance hall.[6] It may have been Sissy's beautiful voice that eventually won the heart of Kunkus, who was considered one of the Wallaga Lake Gum

The Wallaga Lake Gum Leaf Band travelling with members of the Cummeragunja Performers near Balranald, 1935. The driver (second from the left) is Jimmy 'Kunkus' Little senior.

Leaf Band's flashiest performers. Music had been an integral part of mission life for Aboriginal people almost everywhere. Aboriginal people living on missions in that era were greatly inspired by the Christian musical influences imposed upon them by Christian missionaries and managers. The generation of Aboriginal people who were Jimmy's Elders' age could still speak their native tongue relatively fluently, even though missionaries discouraged them from doing so. Jimmy said that his Elders encouraged his generation to speak proper English, because it meant survival in the new world, where their native language was not heard. But they were able to hold onto what cultural knowledge they could. Native languages were not permitted on missions and reserves because they were suspicious of it, so Aboriginal people would speak their language out of the earshot of the mission managers.

When we sang, we sang in English, because we were increasingly influenced by radio, records and picture shows, and travelling shows, and it was well accepted that we must use the English language to communicate with the outside world. If you can imagine, on the weekends – after the men would finish their chores of fruit picking and timber cutting and shearing and all those hard labour jobs – the weekend would be spent making artefacts, by the men and women, and this would be a form of bartering and trade to the town people. And what funds we could make went into helping everyone in that community, as, you must remember, in those days we didn't have government grants, medical – you know, so we had to look after our Elders and children, and this was our way of generating funds, generating goodwill and keeping in touch with the past, and looking into the future.

Gumleaf playing would generally accompany in harmony with the hymnal choruses that were sung – as well, there was blackface minstrelling, along with travelling shows and campfire recitals. The band appeared at football dances, on the back of trucks at district shows and gymkhanas, and at sports picnics on the beach; they would sing Black American spiritualist songs and do traditional dances with sticks and spears. Step dancing, tap dancing, burlesque, clowning, accordion and fiddle playing became a part of their cash-based economy, with them hamming it up as much as they could for their audiences, who were a mixture of White and Black Australians.[7]

My father was a dancer – in terms of traditional dance and show business, vaudevillian dancing – and he was a comedian, a natural comedian and storyteller. As a boy in the audience, I remember watching Dad on stage with a lantern and a little fan, and some crepe paper, and this was fire, on stage with all the lights out and dancing round the fire ... I would see him add charcoal colouring ... like that Al Jolson thing? Blackface, what did they call them? Minstrels. So Dad saw the movie minstrels, and related – I can do that. Mum, on the other hand, would come out in a lovely evening gown, and sing in a clear voice, singing Swiss-type yodelling songs.

The choir made their own costumes and stage curtains with their trusty Singer treadle sewing machine. They took it with them everywhere they travelled.[8] They gained such a widespread reputation that an article about them appeared in the Sydney-based magazine *Pix*.[9] They performed a variety of styles in an assortment of places (including churches), showing off their skills as singers and dancers and as players of a range of musical instruments.[10] These included piano, piano accordion, banjo, guitar, violin and harmonica, as well as the gumleaf, and their music ranged from traditional to modern – but it was rare for traditional Aboriginal songs and musical instruments to feature, and any use of the didgeridoo was unusual in these parts of the country.

The didgeridoo ... really only ever belonged to the Aborigines who came from the northern parts of Australia. But we had our own gumleaf playing and 'whistling' recitals that were frequently accompanied by the Elders of the camp, who sometimes clapped the boomerangs and chanted tunes that they had tried to carry down throughout the ages from our ancestors.

THE ABORIGINAL CHOIR

The Aborigines will give the programme at the Celebration of the 102nd Anniversary of Melbourne's Birthday: English and Aboriginal Songs

IN THE AUSTRALIAN CHURCH, RUSSELL STREET MONDAY EVENING, 31ST MAY 1937

- Cummeragungee Chimes
- Duets and Quartets
- A Harp and Gum Leaf Orchestra
- Playing on Hoop Iron
- All Things turned to Melody, as in Bush Land
- Six Little Native Girls
- The Laughing Nigger
- The Lyre Bird

IN AID OF THE OLD PIONEERS' MEMORIAL FUND
DR JAMES BOOTH Presides

Lecturette by ISAAC SELBY
Doors open at 7.15
Orchestra at 8 o'clock
Body of Church 1/- [Front Seats 2/-] [11]

Kunkus and Sissy's first-born, James Oswald Little, came into the world on 1 March 1937. He was always told that he was born under 'a big old gum tree' on Cummeragunja Mission, along the banks of the Murray River.[12] In those days, it was not unusual for Aboriginal children to be born in such settings and Jimmy Little was proud of the fact that he was delivered by the Yorta Yorta women Elders in such a natural and cultural way.

It was as if my birth had been an indication of what my life as a Yorta Yorta man would become. That is, I would come from out of hardship and toil, and have to learn all about having to survive in a brand-new world, while being cradled by my Aboriginal ways.

The Murray River at Cummeragunja was known as Dhungala to the local Yorta Yorta, who likened their river to the kidneys, filtering and cleansing the lands. The traditional lands identified by the descendants in a native title claim in 1994 lay on both sides of the Murray River from Cohuna to Albury-Wodonga, including towns such as Echuca, Shepparton, Benalla, Corowa and Wangaratta, and extending northwards to just short of Deniliquin.[13] Cummeragunja Mission is in New South Wales, along the Murray River, a couple of kilometres from Barmah in Victoria and 30 kilometres north of Echuca Moama. The mission sits on fertile lands surrounding the river, which is lined with sandy beaches and forests of red gum. When Jimmy was born, the river still provided just enough fresh foods for the families, whose diets at that time mainly relied on the paltry rations doled out by the mission managers.

According to Jimmy, his mother Sissy was a Yorta Yorta woman whose people were freshwater river people and whose totem was the long-necked turtle. In recent years, however, there have been ongoing disputes over who is legally recognised by the Australian legal system as a traditional descendant of the Yorta Yorta nation and who is not. Criticisms were aimed at Jimmy while he was alive, declaring that he was not Yorta Yorta but was in fact Wamba Wamba – whose Country consists of an area that spans both sides of the Murray River and includes the townships of Deniliquin, Moulamein and Swan Hill[14] – but Jimmy always believed that he was Yorta Yorta, connected with the Country where he was born. Although his mother Sissy was born and lived on Wamba Wamba Country before she married, this is not the way he identified. Firstly, because it was not what he was told by his Elders; and secondly, because he never held much faith in the political processes of native title laws imposed upon the people by governments and legal authorities who, in his mind, have failed to understand the intricate relationships Aboriginal people have to land and extended family connections which spread across hundreds of kilometres over time.

When Sissy McGee became Mrs Little, she was marrying a Yuin-Monaro man from Wallaga Lake, an Aboriginal mission on the South Coast of New South Wales. They married at the Baptist Church, Koondrook, Victoria, on Barapa Barapa Country,[15] on 14 December 1935, about a hundred kilometres west of Cummeragunja. Kunkus's Yuin-Monaro Country lies in the south-eastern region of New South Wales, stretching along the coast from Nowra to Eden, then extending back inland along the Southern Tablelands, from Cooma to as far north as Braidwood.

CHAPTER 2

'Homeland'

Homeland Homeland
A treasure chest of gems old and new
Homeland Homeland
A pleasure paradise for me and you

Our land speaks to us in a whisper
There are signs and symbols everywhere
With night and day information
Mother-nature Father-time's loving care

Grandmother moon in all her glory
With her yellow mellow moonbeams at night
While Grandfather's golden ray of sunshine
Gives a warm-hearted bright guiding light

The sweet sounds of early birds are calling
To herald in another newborn day
Awakening all God's creations
From their restful little haven hide away

The landscape is pure and perfume flavoured
By the handwork of God's own design
The free-flowing breeze in the tree tops
Swings and sways with enchanting sounds of chime

The water world's most prized possession
For life on the land within
Mountain streams, rivers to the ocean
With shell, skin, feather, fur and fin

Raindrops add moisture to the sweetness
With freshness like early morning dew
This is what we love and live for
A dreamtime reality come true

Home is truly where the heart is
It's where all life begins and ends
Our paths may be paved with good intentions
But too often too hard to comprehend.

Jimmy's great-grandparents, Sissy's grandparents, were Oswald 'Osley' Ingram and Frances (nee Green). When they were young (in the late nineteenth century), they were among the many Aboriginal fringe dwellers who drifted from missions to stations in search of work, barely getting by, living in makeshift homes, and often finding jobs as domestic help or station hands. Wherever they went, they supplemented their wages and rations by resorting to their traditional hunting skills to make do.[16]

At this time, the Aborigines Protection Board (APB) was setting up missions all over Victoria and New South Wales, taking control of the lives of Aboriginal people – deciding where they should live, where they should work and, above all, teaching them the 'arts of white civilization'.[17] Oswald and Frances Ingram had been living on the outskirts of Swan Hill, Victoria, where in 1879 their daughter Janet (Sissy's mother) was born.[18]

While Oswald and Frances were on Cummeragunja, Oswald got into a bitter dispute with the mission manager, complaining, in 1899, that the rations they received were unsatisfactory.[19] This resulted in them being moved on to Mount Tulla Station, probably because Oswald was now marked down as an agitator, and not because he chose to leave Cummeragunja.[20] In those times, the term agitator was given to just about anyone who asked for things that a manager considered unreasonable, whereupon a police officer would remove the 'agitator' without notice or enquiry.[21] Janet's future husband, Ernest McGee, was also considered to be a troublemaker at Cummeragunja. In his case, he dared to submit a farming land requisition, which was surprisingly accepted,[22] even though he remained defiant, playing an active role in writing letters and petitions at Moonacullah Mission,[23] insisting they replace their current teacher[24] with Thomas Shadrach James (1859–1946).[25]

Ernest McGee was the son of Johanna Higgs and George McGee, as his death certificate indicates. Very little is known of Johanna Higgs, but Ernest's father, George, was thought to be an Irish immigrant who worked briefly as a station manager but died tragically in 1903 from drowning in the Billabong Creek, near Wanganella, New South Wales, apparently by his own hands.[26]

Ernest, it seems, was abandoned at an early age by his parents George and Johanna and was raised by the Joachim family on Moonacullah, where he was commonly referred to as the 'black Irishman'. Jimmy's earliest memory of his grandfather Ernest was that he was fully Irish; however, the records document Ernest as being 'quarter-caste' Aboriginal.

Like many young men living and working on Moonacullah and Cummeragunja missions during that era, Ernest farmed the land well into the 1890s before he submitted his land requisition form. Ernest found work as a boundary rider at Mount Tulla Station, a property on the outskirts of Moulamein, a quiet little town on the Edwards River, 160 kilometres north of Cummeragunja.

He arrived at Mount Tulla Station about the same time as the Ingrams, with Janet Ingram taking up work there as a domestic servant. Janet and Ernest McGee married on 4 May 1901 in the Moulamein Post Office.[27] Their first child, Henry, was born in 1901, and they went on to have twelve more children, with barely a year between each one. The youngest of thirteen children, Frances (Sissy, Jimmy's mother) was named after Janet's mother, Frances Ingram, but according to Jimmy, because she was the baby in the family, she was called Sissy. As large as his mother's family was, Jimmy would hold the names of his twelve uncles and aunts in his head, even though he barely knew them.

Let's see now, there was Aunty Bella McGee, Uncle Leslie, Uncle Osley, Aunty Grace, Uncle Ernie, Aunty Ethel, Uncle Conley, Uncle Henry, Aunty Dina, Aunty Lena, Uncle Samuel, Aunty Lily and then my mum, Frances McGee, who would later be better known as and called Sissy, because she had been the youngest girl in the family.

Jimmy's mother Sissy was born in 1921 near Barham,[28] a little town on the Murray River approximately 120 kilometres west of Cummeragunja. After Sissy was born, her parents Ernest and Janet returned to live on Cummeragunja. By then the mission manager was J. G. Danvers, with whom many Aboriginal people had grievances.[29] Unfortunately, worse times lay ahead for the family.

In 1937, the year Jimmy was born on Cummeragunja, Danvers was replaced by A. J. McQuiggan, who had been dismissed from his position as superintendent of Kinchela Aboriginal Boys' Home due to repeated complaints about his brutal beatings of the boys.[30]

McQuiggan brought with him arrogance, threats and violence.[31] The new homes he promised to build turned out to be nothing more than two-roomed slums made from mill rubbish and tin sheets, with wooden shutters in place of windows.[32] The pumping plant Jimmy's family and the other Cummeragunja residents had ordered ten months previously was yet to arrive,[33] and their drinking water was the same water used for the stock, which was very often contaminated. Even the milk from their dairy cows was no longer safe to drink.[34] McQuiggan further taunted them by taking the endowment cheques from the women, removing his cut and then doling out what was left. When residents decided to take their complaints to the board, they asked William Cooper, a shearer and self-educated man who came from Cummeragunja[35] but now lived in Melbourne, to represent them. When McQuiggan learned of this, he further punished the residents[36] by withholding rations and handing out rancid cuts of meat, and flour riddled with weevils.[37]

At this time, tuberculosis was sweeping through the community, sending many babies and elderly people to their graves, including Jimmy's siblings Madeline Elizabeth (in 1938) and Ernest (in 1939), both of them dying in their infancy. The tuberculosis spread rapidly, hitting the news in the *Daily Telegraph*.[38] To the readers in Sydney and elsewhere, these deaths may have just been a number, but for Jimmy they included his sister and brother, and their deaths affected him for a long time. This is probably why Jimmy found that his parents doted on him for so long.[39]

When William Cooper wrote his letters and petitions to the New South Wales APB on behalf of the people of Cummeragunja, all of them were ignored. Tensions continued to soar, but the people never lost faith in Cooper. Naturally, they did lose confidence in the APB, and their frustration led to a series of protests. On 3 February 1939, approximately 200 of the 300 residents of Cummeragunja organised a strike and walked off the station, demanding that McQuiggan be replaced by a more compassionate manager. The following day, John (Jack) Patten, Aboriginal activist and journalist, was arrested and removed from the mission after trying to address the local people, who had already crossed the river and set up camp in Victoria.[40]

Their strike lasted nine months, but unfortunately it had little effect on the New South Wales Government, which left the problem to the APB. The APB responded with a promise to the residents that if they returned, there would be a full inquiry into their complaints and there would be no reprisals from McQuiggan. With food in short supply and the winter weather taking its toll, they agreed to come back and waited another five weeks to see if any action would be taken by the APB. No inquiry took place and McQuiggan responded by further spoiling their supplies, so a second walk-off was staged. This time, only eighty residents took part.[41] The strike continued until such time as the APB convinced the government to withhold their food rations and to ban their children from attending school; by October 1939 the strikers' spirits had been broken.[42]

Jimmy was far too young to remember being carried off in the arms of his mother and father during the 1939 Cummeragunja Walk-off, but he retained strong feelings on how the strikes affected everyone.

Yeah, well, I was only two years old, and what can I say other than in some ways I was there at the time when things were not happy and I'm pleased that I come from a strong family of traditional fighters, even though, myself, I'm very passive. But I do often wonder about the times that my mum and her parents had to go through in order to deal with the government and racism back in those days, and I am amazed, but also proud of the way they handled it, with dignity and strength of mind.

Perhaps the appalling conditions at Cummeragunja, along with the strike, had more of an influence on Jimmy than he appreciated. In the years of hardships ahead, his parents Kunkus and Sissy continued to travel from place to place, with Jimmy in tow, just as Sissy's parents Ernest and Janet had done before them. The strike drove many young Aboriginal families of Sissy and Kunkus's generation to leave Cummeragunja for good. A few stayed on, while others moved to nearby towns like Shepparton,[43] such as his Aunty Bella McGee, who was thirty-six years old at the time of the strike. Jimmy recalls where many of his aunts and uncles moved following the strike.

Today I have just as many relatives living in Victoria as I do in New South Wales. For example, Aunty Bella married William Atkinson, and they are one of the largest Aboriginal families in Victoria today. Uncle Leslie married Freda Weston and raised their family around Shepparton and Mooroopna, while Aunty Ethel, who moved to Barham in 1939, married William Galway and had a large family of fifteen children. Others went to various parts of New South Wales and so on.

Kunkus and Sissy, with a very young Jimmy, went to live briefly with his Aunty Grace, who was married to a non-Aboriginal man, George Barton, who worked for the Post Master General in Goulburn, New South Wales. The Bartons had a large family of eighteen children, so Kunkus and Sissy set up a place of their own in Goulburn, remaining there for Jimmy's preschool years.

I was still Mum and Dad's only child at that stage. I'm not sure what kind of work Dad did up there, but, knowing him, he'd work anywhere he could, doing a lot of casual or handy work, like fruit picking or tending to other people's gardens. One of my earliest memories of living in Goulburn was waiting with Mum for Dad to come home. It was always dark when he got home, and he'd come home carrying a big bag of mixed biscuits. Well, to me it was a giant bag of biscuits. He was like that, always coming home to me and Mum with a present or two. And I remember sitting on the bed between Mum and Dad while he told Mum all the happenings of the day, and I was getting my cuddles and my free go at the biscuits in the big bag on the bed, and I thought it was just delicious. It was very special to me.

Having lost his brother and sister to the tuberculosis, Jimmy remained an only child for a few years and remembers playing with his older cousins, who allowed him to be a mischievous lad who got away with things.

I remember being around at the flats where Aunty Gracie lived. I was sitting out the front by myself – the buildings are still there too, incidentally, the ones I remember – when the baker came by in a horse-drawn cart, much like the milkmen would do, and the iceman, in those days. He pulled up a door or so away and left a loaf of bread on the steps, which was the fashion at the time – the butchers, the bakers and the ice people would knock on the door and then leave the groceries or the goods right there. For some reason or other, I whizzed up to the step and moved the bread from one door to the other, and just then a little girl, around about my age or a little older, came outside and spotted me, took me by surprise. When she raced back into the house, telling the family that the baker had called, I took off and ran inside so I wouldn't get caught.

Jobs were scarce around Goulburn, so when Kunkus's brothers told him there was timber work back on the South Coast of New South Wales, he decided to join them. Jimmy would have been about five years old when the Little family moved to the coast, to saltwater country. It was there in Nowra, New South Wales, that Jimmy's brother Freddy was born in 1941 and where Jimmy would finally live with his father's people, the Yuin and Monaro clans; Jimmy would try to remember their names.

Now there was a big mob of relatives all along the South Coast too. Everyone had nicknames. For example, my dad's name was Kunkus and his brothers were Pickelo (Jack) and Sutt, who was Eddie (Charles) Little. Then there was Uncle Darlo, who was Uncle William, and Uncle Bardi, who was Uncle Walter, and a whole lot of others. Other names I can recall were Uncles Jubbi, Nurrie, Lulli, Target, Ponjo, Bul, Bing, Goonja, Bunyin, Ceciloe, Dosh, Sungo and Jopie, and Aunties Choonky, Dubs and Chudda. Goodness knows what their proper names were. Many of the names were not necessarily traditional Aboriginal names, but sometimes highlighted a person's individual character, like Aunty Chudda, for example, who acquired the name because she had a habit of saying she 'shoulda' done this, or 'shoulda' done that.

When the timber mill work came to a halt, Jimmy's family briefly headed back to Cummeragunja, where Sissy gave birth to Jimmy's sister Betty in 1944. They remained on the move, heading to Shepparton in Victoria, and then right across the Riverina area, working as fruit and vegetable pickers. This meant living in tents and makeshift camps with all the other Aboriginal families travelling and working and doing the same things they did, working on the farms.

Meanwhile World War II was raging overseas and Australians were experiencing the effects at home. One of the farms they worked and lived on was near Tatura, a place where several internment camps were set up for the purposes of housing German, Italian and Japanese internees.[44] Tatura was 19 kilometres west of Shepparton and 16 kilometres south of Mooroopna. Kunkus and Sissy set up camp with their three young children in one of the fields just south of the Goulburn River. The living conditions were makeshift, but this never bothered Jimmy, who appreciated that it was his home and was glad to be living among his extended family.

I remember the camps we lived in. Our old house, or humpy, whatever you want to call it, was made of chaff, corn or flour bags sewn together, suspended on wooden frames, and plastered over with papier-mâché, with old used kerosene tins serving as a roof. They were warm and comfortable, but also, very ... what can you say ... very flammable. We had to make our own candles for lighting back in those days. We had no electricity or running water.

One night a fire spark caught the old hut, and it was so quick that everybody raced outside. 'Oh, the old place is on fire!' In the rush and panic, Mum turned around to Dad. 'Where's Jimmy?' Before they realised, Uncle Foxy had already run back inside, picking me up just before the roof fell in. And poor old Uncle Foxy [Ernest McGee Jr] come out burnt – his hair and his eyelashes singed all over from grabbing and protecting me. Although we all laughed about it, it was an incident that made you think, gee, you know, that was a close call – I was destined to live longer for a reason.

The fire did not deter Kunkus or Sissy from continuing their work in the fields and raising their three young children; they had little choice, to be honest. They would not dare to complain, for fear of punishment from the Aboriginal Welfare Board (AWB),[45] who were constantly looking out for Aboriginal children to place in institutions. There were no schools nearby to speak of and certainly no child-minding centres where they were. Jimmy remembered helping his parents with their jobs of ploughing the earth, picking fruit and laying down irrigation canals. All this seemed very normal to Jimmy, who remembers those days as 'fun' and 'loving', with always something nice to eat.

Luckily for us, the irrigation canals would fill up with crawfish, and they were delicious. We would go down, and tie meat on a cotton string and hold it and fish crawfish out of the little channels. We'd pull them up slowly when we felt them taking, and we'd have a wire netting, a basket, we'd put underneath quietly and then catch them like that and boil them, and they were delicious. But only the big ones; the little ones we'd let go. That was fun, because we always had mushrooms and fish, crawfish, fresh fruit, fresh vegetables, and, in lots of cases, fresh milk in those farming areas.

Kunkus and Sissy knew the risk of sending their children away to school, where the AWB could take them away. Instead, they kept Jimmy, Freddy and Colin close by, despite the fact that they lived and worked under such trying conditions. They knew, of course, this meant that the children might miss out on an early education. Leaving them in the care of someone else or calling for a doctor when their children were sick was not an option, though, even when Freddy ate a pesticide-infested tomato.

Apparently they'd put insect spray on the fruit and veggies, and somehow Freddy must have got hold of one of the tomatoes, and fell into a fit. Mum was nearby, but he was in Dad's arms when he started going out to it. Dad panicked and gave up trying to revive him, thinking, you know, we've lost him. I was standing right by too. But Mum took Freddy off Dad and slapped his face and brought him around – shocked him back into his senses – and he came out of the fit. That was frightening. It all happened so quickly, but, yeah, it's just as well Mum acted as she did. Dad was not a cruel man, so the idea that he'd ever strike one of his kids was a bit too much for him, I suppose. But everyone was okay, and so there was nothing else to do but get on with it.

With many Australian workers now overseas fighting in the war, Aboriginal people benefitted from the increased need for seasonal workers. Kunkus was seldom, if ever, out of work, travelling from town to town and camping in humpies. He and his family lived partly off rations and partly off the produce they farmed. One time, Kunkus, Sissy, Jimmy, Freddy and Colin were in Mooroopna when they watched several truckloads of Japanese internees driving by.

A couple of trucks full of Japanese people passed us by while we were eating our lunch in the park one day. Although they were in a covered truck, they had been looking out and waving. They all seemed to be happy, just waving to the people going along. It was a new sight to me, because it was the first time I ever saw Japanese people, [and I was] wondering what they all were doing in that truck and where were they going.

Another curious wartime memory for Jimmy was when his parents went to Koondrook, in Victoria, for work. He and his cousins, who were mostly older than he was, spotted a group of Australian soldiers at the railway station.

The train came right into Koondrook, where it terminated, and we saw all the young soldiers. It must have been the end of the war. They were all in uniform and seemed to be jolly and happy. Me and all the cousins were on the platform while the soldiers threw big handfuls of pennies, showering us.

With the fruit and vegetable picking season coming to a close, it was time for Kunkus to do a bit of woodcutting in the Barham forest, just as his father-in-law, Ernest McGee, had done back in 1921. Jimmy never cared much for Koondrook, perhaps because when they were there, he would rarely get to spend time with his father, who worked at the timber mill all day.

Dad would go to work in the dark and come home in the dark, because he walked to work – and sometimes that was miles – and walked home, so by the time he'd go, and get back, it was kind of in the dark. I would get up and he would have the radio on, the old wireless, and would be listening, particularly in the morning, to country music, hillbilly music. All the early cowboys of Australia and America were always on the radio and I soaked all of that up.

For the first time in Jimmy's short life, he felt uncomfortable. In Koondrook, he had a curious sense that he was living in strange country.[46] There was no way of explaining this, but he felt unwelcome there; he had the sense he was in a place he did not belong, and he felt this especially after an ominous storm blew over them.

I remember one time playing with a bunch of kids there. Then one afternoon the sky got real dark, like a big storm was brewing, and we were all called inside to weather the storm. All the kids were rounded up. 'Come inside now, big storm' – you know, that kind of thing. I don't remember hearing any rain or thunder or lightning, it just went awfully dark, pitch black like midnight, and there was a stillness, there was a calmness, and it was the weirdest thing I ever saw. When it passed over – I don't know how long it was, it wasn't all that long, maybe twenty or thirty minutes – the sky cleared, and we went outside to have a look. A lot of things were blown about; it was like a dry storm. There was rubbish sort of everywhere, like street rubbish and yard rubbish, and things blown around the place. Apparently nobody was hurt, but it was the weirdest storm I've ever witnessed, and I've never seen one like it since.

Jimmy was relieved when the woodcutting season finished and the Little family could leave Koondrook behind and go back to Cummeragunja. The strike had brought about many changes there. The mission manager, McQuiggan, had finally been dismissed, and the rations were slightly improved, but the most noticeable change was the decline in numbers of people living on Cummeragunja. Many of the old people were now long gone and the younger members of the McGee family had married and moved away – the Atkinsons, Galways, Westons, Woodings, Bartons, Harrisons, Ryans and Taylors.

Sadly, Jimmy's grandparents – Ernest and Janet McGee – had passed on and were no longer there. Janet had died in Echuca Hospital of carcinoma of the stomach on 18 October 1939. She was sixty years old and had been diagnosed with the disease three years prior to her death. Echuca Hospital was 35 kilometres from Cummeragunja – a long way to go for treatment – and she would never have been allowed to sit in the cabin of the truck, but only allowed to sit in the dray. This was a firm order by McQuiggan, who insisted that no one be allowed to join him in the cabin of the truck.

> Even native women, known to be tubercular, are required to sit on the back of the truck, in the cold and wet.[47]

Janet died the same month that the strikers returned to Cummeragunja. She did not live to see the day that McQuiggan was kicked off the station, in February 1940, but her husband Ernest, who had been a source of agitation to McQuiggan, survived long enough to see the victory; he died later that year in Moama, however.[48]

For the brief time they returned to Cummeragunja, Jimmy attended the Cummeragunja schoolhouse; his brother Freddy and Colin were not yet old enough for school. With the years passing quickly, and the return of the Australian soldiers, work became even more scarce for Aboriginal people, particularly for the residents of Cummeragunja, who were tarnished with the reputation of being troublemakers who would most likely 'walk-off' the job at a moment's notice. So, while they were there, all Kunkus could hope for was to tend gardens in the private homes of the people who lived in Echuca or Moama, more than 35 kilometres away. With Kunkus receiving a pay that was barely enough to keep them together, it became time to leave again, especially now that Sissy was pregnant with their fourth child.[49]

Sissy and Kunkus might have stayed on, living with Sissy's large and extended family at Cummeragunja, had it not been for the upheaval and adversity they'd encountered. Now, at seven years old,

Jimmy and his family were leaving Yorta Yorta Country for good, and Jimmy would grow up not knowing much about the family he left behind, although he tried catching up with them later in life.

I knew the older women in my mother's family, like her sisters Isabella Atkinson, Grace Barton and Diane Wooding, who apparently went away early in life – I don't know the circumstances – but I did meet Aunty Di years later in Coonamble with her husband and some of my cousins for the first time, which was quite a thrill. But when Mum and Dad moved to the South Coast, Nowra to be exact, my mother's sister Lena and two brothers Colin [Conley] and Ernie Uncle Foxy also came to live with us. So I grew up really only knowing them well from my mother's side, of which there were thirteen brothers and sisters.

It would not be until Jimmy was in his sixties that he would search the archives for his family tree, seeing how far back he could go, to find out about his Yorta Yorta people. Throughout the years, he would meet with some of his extended family members, who occasionally came to his shows, or he would call in on them whenever possible. While he loved reconnecting with family and talking about their Elders and the Country they grew up on, they, like him, only had vague memories of their Elders, as many of them had passed on since Jimmy was a child. When he could, though, he would visit the Country down at Cummeragunja, and reach out to their spirits on the land, which he believed still remained there.

Leaving Cummeragunja again, Jimmy's family headed north to Uranquinty, a little town 17 kilometres south of Wagga Wagga, where Sissy gave birth to Colin at the local hospital, in 1943.

When work continued to elude them once again, they journeyed back to the South Coast, to Kunkus's Country, the land that belongs to the Yuin-Monaro people, where Jimmy would begin a new chapter in his life, as a saltwater person.

CHAPTER 3

'Woorigee'

Paperbark, spotted-gum and tea-trees
Line the pathway that led towards home
From the corner crossroad by-way
Right there at 'Greenwell' Point road.
The old yellow bus would stop here
Where we'd play in-wait for Aunty Jane
She'd come home from town with groceries
For the families down 'Woorigee' Lane.
Shopping was a special occasion
For us kids way back in those days
It was almost as good as Christmas
In its own sweet memorable way.
I can only just now imagine
What the grown-ups saw back then
As they watched our fun-filled faces
Stock-up kitchen cupboards again.
Of course, there were always our lollies
Biscuits and tins of canned fruit
Honey, jam and peanut butter
Home-made damper with treacle too.

Frances Peters-Little

After the rain we'd go hunting
For rabbits and mushrooms galore
Blackberries, sweet cherries delicious
We never had time to be bored.
Summertime we'd all go swimming
Near the swampland where the swans would fly
There were frogs, tadpoles and turtles
And the odd slippery eels going by.
There were cranes, ducks and waterhen
Kookaburras, magpies and crow
Pee-wees, willy-wagtails, butcher birds
And each one would put on a show.
Mondays to Fridays were school days
Saturday, Sunday were fun days
Discipline assured there were rule days
And no time for acting the fool days.
Weekends we'd all go to the movies
They were called picture-shows back then
A serial, two features and a cartoon,
Not thinking those days would ever end.
If I could be granted three wishes
For me and my family and friends
To my 'Lord' I'd forever be grateful
If we could all live those days again.

The Williams, Mumblers and Hickeys
Carpenters, Connollys and Coombes
Chapmans, Kennedys and Perrys
And McLeods to name a few.

Bonds, Littles and Mundys
Ardlers, Wrights and Browns
Ashbys, Cruses and Stewarts
Good neighbours from all round town.
And blessed are my siblings
With whom these tears I shed
Colin, Betty and Monica
And our beloved brother Fred.
We had madness, gladness and sadness
But little would I care to change
About our early childhood
Living down 'Woorigee' Lane.
Most elders have passed on now
But their love and spirits remain
In a legacy we share together
From home down 'Woorigee' Lane.

Permanently moving to the New South Wales South Coast was a homecoming for Kunkus Little, who could trace his family tree back to the early days of White settlement in the region. He enjoyed telling Jimmy about these ancestors. Kunkus's great-grandmother was Elizabeth Turner, who was born in 1857 at Dignam Creek, and was described as being a servant at Wagonga Farm, from the very young age of eight years. Her father was an Englishman, Thomas Turner of Lincolnshire, who married Mary Ann Koma,[50] a 'full-blooded' Aboriginal woman from Dry River.[51] Elizabeth Turner married a William Penrith, who was born in the United Kingdom in 1802 and died in Bega, New South Wales, in 1892. Their daughter Eliza was Kunkus's mother. Before Eliza married Kunkus's father, she had a former marriage to Walter Brierly, and had four children with him (Walter, William, Sara and Jane). In her marriage to her second husband, John Edward Little, she had four more children (John 'Jack', Rebecca, Kunkus and Charles 'Eddie').

The New South Wales South Coast not only became the home for Kunkus and Sissy, but also for Sissy's sister Lena (who had married Kunkus's brother Jack), and her brothers Foxy and Conley came to join her there, too. Needless to say, the constant search for full-time, steady employment remained the focus of their concerns, especially now that Sissy had given birth to their youngest child, Monica, in Nowra; fortunately, though, Kunkus did find steady work.

> Dad found work locally with timber cutting, fruit picking and different kinds of odd jobs on the South Coast, New South Wales, around Nowra, where Dad took up truck driving for the next eight to nine years in a stable situation of employment.[52]

The first place the family settled back in Yuin-Monaro Country was Woorigee Lane, an Aboriginal campsite just south of Terara and five kilometres east of the township of Nowra. Woorigee was the Aboriginal word for 'peppermint tree' but non-Aboriginal people called the area Worrigee, which has since become a suburb of Nowra. The Aboriginal families who lived at Woorigee considered it a peaceful and harmonious place. The Nowra Council, on the other hand, argued that these people should be forced to live on the mission at Roseby Park, which was established in 1900 on Orient Point, a further 23 kilometres east of Nowra. Some Aboriginal families stood strong against this pressure and remained at Woorigee, because they wanted their independence. There were also practical reasons to stay. They were closer to the farms they worked on, and their lives were much nourished by working the farms, as they could eat the fruit and vegetables they picked, and drink fresh milk from the dairies. The farmers also preferred them to be living at Woorigee, as here they provided a readily available workforce.

Living in Woorigee made it possible for the residents to walk into town or catch the bus whenever they wanted, to go to the pictures, or attend a regular school instead of the mission school set up on Roseby Park. Many of the children growing up in Woorigee attended Terara Public School, which temporarily became a denominational school attached to St John's Church of England. Several Aboriginal children attended this small school along with the children of the farmers in the area.

Jimmy and his brothers and sisters had fond memories of school, even though they had a five-kilometre walk to get there and had to walk the five kilometres back home again at the end of the day.

Not everyone had pushbikes in those days; it was kind of a luxury, as cars are a luxury. We would go to town by walking, or catch the community bus, and get the bus home. But when somebody did get a bike, you finished up having to all take it in turns riding to get to school. At Terara school, I got my share of the cane and chastising for being late and for staying away – absent from school with no reasons other than I didn't want to go. A lot of kids got the cane for different things, and that was my reason for being disciplined, just being, not lazy, but not fully attending school. I liked school, but there were times and days that I'd say, 'Oh, I don't want to go today,' and I'd stay home and try and cook up an excuse for the teacher, and then when the teacher realised that I was being undisciplined, we'd get the cane. It really hurt too.

Despite these bouts of rebellion, Jimmy did quite well at school.

In my class at Terara, there were six of us – four boys and two girls. One of the girls was our teacher's daughter, Marian, and naturally she used to always be top of the class in the exams, and next to her would be Toby – he was a whiz with maths and many other subjects – and I used to always come third. Then the rest of the class would be four, five and six. One year I was so determined to see how good I could be in my exams, I came first. I can't think of the year, but I was top of the class that year, and in some ways, I guess they were surprised, but I just wanted to prove to myself that I could do exactly what the other students were doing; it's just that I wasn't always pushing to be top of the class. I was happy to be one of the better class members in terms of knowledge, general knowledge, but this year I wanted to prove something, and I did.

He remembers his first break in the school drama.

Some weeks before[hand], everyone would be chosen to play a role in some play, like *Snow White and the Seven Dwarves*, and things like that. You'd put your hand up to say what character you wanted to play. I played a few characters. I was a page in one show, and I was the voice behind the mirror when the wicked Queen would ask: 'Mirror, mirror on the wall, who's the fairest of them all?'

Jimmy's early memories of wanting to perform to an audience were shaping up very early in his life.

I wanted to build a little treehouse right behind the house where we were living in Woorigee. I climbed up there and I took a few boards up and a hammer and nails, and it was just a little, what they call, cubbyhouse. Dad helped me to make it secure. It was fun just sitting up there. I remember sitting up there a lot after dinner, up in my little cubbyhouse, overlooking the house we lived in. I remember singing, singing to a sea of faces, an imaginary audience. I did that a lot, even when I was walking to school and walking home, or hunting rabbits. I would walk along singing and imagining this great big audience. I even made my own little guitar out of an oval-type herring tin nailed on a piece of board, and telephone wires. We stripped the old telephone wires from the rubbish tip. I would wind them around a nail on both ends and it would give me a jingling sound, and it was my pretend guitar.

Unfortunately, his treehouse stage was to come down with a fiery thump.

Ah yes, that treehouse had a tin-type floor, and I thought it was great. I was up there with a cousin, and someone else, I think – I think three of us were up there. I made this little fire up in the treehouse. No walls, just a floor. Just beginning to enjoy this little campfire up in the trees – I always liked to do something different – but the limb broke. So my little cubbyhouse and myself, and my companions, didn't fall very far, and nobody really got hurt, but we certainly laughed for days about it. Tumbling out of the tree, and the little fire went everywhere; lucky! – we could've really got hurt.

As the eldest of his brothers and sisters, Jimmy always felt a responsibility to help his parents.

Being the eldest in the family by a few years, I was capable of helping Mum and Dad in little duties around home, and to me it was natural for all the kids of my generation; we were all kind of active in doing things with our parents in domestic ways and, in the case of our dads, when our dads would go to work, we would gather firewood and carry water and do things at home while our dads were away. That just helped the family, because we knew Dad would come home tired and Mum would have a great meal cooking, and I always felt that I was the little man around the house helping in that situation, so it was just a joy to be able to feel like family.

I enjoyed making bottles, like making the baby bottles for my brothers and sisters, washing up and tidying the house if Mum was in town shopping, like a babysitter would do, and it was kind of fun. I'm glad I did that rather than just play, play, play, which I had plenty of time to do. There were no real restrictions, other than doing our chores and being respectful around adult things, and being mindful of being generally a good child, whatever that meant. We just wanted to be liked and appreciated, I suppose, for our efforts and our duties.

Jimmy's mother Sissy and the other women in Woorigee worked tirelessly, often with their children in tow. Even in those instances, Jimmy and the others found ways to have fun.

The council used to make big dams for waterholes, for cattle to drink. When it rained, the dams would fill up, and that was fresh water for the cattle and the sheep and the horses. At different times Mum and the Aunties would take all the washing down and make a fire and boil the clothes and do our washing down there and hang it out on bushes and along the fence, like a washday; and we'd have meals down there. When I say 'down there', it's only, I don't know, a few hundred yards away from the house, depending on how far the dams were away. So, we'd be playing there as well, and sometimes even swimming in there, in the man-made dams, while our mums were washing – making a fun day out of it as well as a workday. Or down the creek, whatever the case may be, but there was always a way of getting clean clothes and having a wash ourselves. Swimming was a great pastime in the warm weather. We always had nice little creeks down nearby in Woorigee where we would go and just swim and have a great time. We had so much freedom, and yet we still had our chores to do – then, after that, we were able to please ourselves what we did during the day.

Jimmy also enjoyed the times with his father, Kunkus, and their dogs, hunting or foraging for foods.

Hunting rabbits around Nowra was one of our favourite pastimes. We always had half a dozen dogs. After the rain they [rabbits] would come out of their burrows and go into blackberry bushes and into logs and places and it was easy to get them out of there with the dogs. And then we would chase them with sticks and cripple them and knock them out, and skin them and bring them home, and we had meat, along with our mushrooms and all that – fresh veggies, like tomatoes and potatoes and carrots and lettuce, you name it. We were healthy kids back then.

Hard work was a constant for the people of Woorigee, but they made the best of it. The biggest source of income for Aboriginal people was bean picking, shared between the men and the women. Bean picking started at dawn and finished late in the afternoon – sun, rain and mud notwithstanding. When they had to stand up to pick, their backs paid a heavy price, and their usefulness was short lived, so it was preferable to crawl along the lines of beans or pick in a seated position. Even the backbreaking work of bean picking was viewed by Jimmy with his customary optimism. It was that optimism that Jimmy would always cling to at those times when it was clearly tough and unjust for those around him. This eternal optimism would become a source of frustration for some, though; they thought Jimmy should complain more, be angrier and stop being so forgiving of others.

Jimmy's happy and carefree life came to an unexpected end in 1950. One day his mother Sissy cut her finger on an oyster shell – nothing much, just a small cut – but tetanus developed. Within a matter of days, she passed away, at the young age of twenty-nine. Jimmy was just thirteen years old.

In my own deep feeling for the loss of Mum, I used to pour my emotions out in playing guitar and singing songs that reflected better days – the songs that my mum used to teach me, I would sing them. As I poured my emotions into song and music, to bring pleasure to others, I found it was a kind of medicine. I felt I needed to express my love of life, and what blessings I had, even though my family had been disrupted. I was reaching out for affection, appreciation or understanding. All these emotions made me look a bit harder at myself, analyse what the future might hold.

The circumstances of Sissy's death and burial were overwhelming for Jimmy and his family. The AWB offered no assistance because the family lived at Woorigee and not on the mission. So, Kunkus desperately took on extra work to raise enough money for a burial. For one job he lined up, he didn't have the money he needed to buy petrol, so, out of desperation, he tried filling his truck with some other sort of fuel. The petrol tank exploded, leaving Kunkus with severe burns to a large part of his body; he was hospitalised before he could even bury his wife. Eventually Sissy was buried in the Aboriginal cemetery at Roseby Park, where today most of the graves are unmarked and the grounds are unkempt.

Jimmy's mother's death was a turning point in his life. To add to the family's collective grief, Kunkus was painfully aware that without Sissy, his children were in danger of being taken away from him by the AWB and fostered out or institutionalised.

Seasonal work took Kunkus up and down the coast, so he called on his stepsister Jane to take care of his children while he was away. Jimmy could have stayed with his Aunty Jane but, instead, he joined his father bean picking while his younger brothers and sisters stayed behind and finished school.

Aunty Jane was a real matriarch, not only to our family but for all the community. She was the representative, the spokesperson. She fought the Welfare and tried to stop them from taking the children away and putting them into the Bomaderry children's home.

Bomaderry Aboriginal Children's Home is located in the town of Bomaderry, situated on the other side of the Shoalhaven River from Nowra. The home was established in 1908 by the United Aborigines Mission and, although it was supposedly independent of the AWB, it was notorious for taking children away from their families. Instead of caring for the so-called 'neglected children', it served as a temporary shelter for children before they were fostered out to White families or sent to institutions such as the Kinchela Boys Home or the Cootamundra Domestic Training Home for Aboriginal Girls. Kunkus's children were fortunate to escape being placed in Bomaderry children's home. Kunkus's brother Jack Little and his partner Lena McGee (Sissy's sister) had two of their children, Ian and Harold, taken away and sent to Kinchela. Jimmy's cousin Harold describes his experience at Kinchela.

> I was about five or six when my mum passed away. The Welfare just come in, and police, and just grabbed us. She was still on the bed with a blanket over her. She passed away that night when they grabbed us. And never even brought us back for her funeral. Oh, there was a big mob there, but they just come in and just grabbed us. Everyone was crying outside. Like it was only a little track. Little dirt track that led into the bush, where they come and dragged us out. I also had a brother, who hid under the

bed, trying to hide. But they went under and grabbed him. I remember him biting someone. And they just dragged us out and put us into an old car and took us to Bomaderry children's home. Our father, Jack Little, couldn't do nothing, because the police and the Welfare was there.[53]

Jimmy realised how lucky he and his brothers and sisters were to escape from being taken. He had never known his Aunty Rebecca (Kunkus's sister), who had been removed from her family by the AWB at the age of eighteen to work as a domestic for White families in Glebe, Mosman and Singleton. She had been allowed to return to Wallaga Lake in early 1928 and married Walter Stewart and had a daughter she called Sarah, but tragically she died the following year.

Jimmy understood the fear in those times, especially as a child. Their fears were as real as their parents'. They had very little control over what the authorities could do to them. Jimmy might have thought he was lucky to escape Woorigee and live with his father and Uncles further down south, with his grandmother Eliza in Wallaga Lake, but the threat of having his family torn apart by the AWB followed them.

CHAPTER 4

'Round the Campfires of Old Wallaga Lake'

Wallaga Lake is here by the Ocean
Where the hilltops and valleys are renowned
We travel up and down the Princes Highway
From Eden to old Nowra town
Proud we are the Wallaga Lake warriors
Descendants from the Yuin Tribal Clan
Grandfather was a true and trusty tracker
While my dad was a-minstrel music man

The Harrisons, the Thomases and Andys
The Hoskins, and Littles all relate
To mission days we all spent together
Round the campfires of old Wallaga Lake
Work occupation was a mixture
Of seasonal and part-time labouring chores
Dairy farms, timber mills and fishing
They were good times had by one and all

Narooma, Tilba Tilba and Bermagui
Still bathe in the sunlight every day
When the soft sea-breezes blowing
It will often steal your heart away
The Moores, Mumblers and Mundys
The Stewarts and the Walkers all relate
To mission days we all spent together
Round the campfires of old Wallaga Lake

The spirits of our loved ones are with us
Inspiring what we will not forsake
The future for our Yuin generation
From the dreamtime of old Wallaga Lake
Behold our beloved Gulaga Mountain
Ceremonial, sacred and serene
Symbolic of the beauty all around her
The land, the sky and the sea

The Penriths, Parsons and Pickallas
The Montas, the Hammonds all relate
To mission days we all spent together
Round the campfires of old Wallaga Lake
The Carters, Chapmans and the Campbells
The Peppers, and Priestleys all relate
To mission days we all spent together
Round the campfires of old Wallaga Lake

The Johnsons, Darcys and the Fosters
The Mullets and McLeod's all relate

To mission days we all spent together
Round the campfires of old Wallaga Lake

At Wallaga Lake Jimmy left behind his childhood and took on the responsibilities of a young man. He also learned more about his Yuin-Monaro culture, because it was Kunkus's Country, black duck country,[54] the place of his South Coast ancestral roots. It was also the place where he would continue to heal his sorrows through music.

Jimmy's father Kunkus had been born to John and Eliza Little on the Wallaga Lake Aboriginal Reserve, just up from Bermagui and near the sacred mountain Gulaga,[55] where the young Kunkus and his brothers spent time climbing and hunting, fishing and farming oysters at Wallaga Lake. Back in his own Country, Kunkus Little, along with his brothers Jack and Eddie, and his thirteen-year-old son Jimmy, would travel long distances up and down the coast, bean picking, milking cows or working in the timber yards.

> I did a number of labouring jobs. I followed Dad into the timber mill industry, as a rouseabout. The youngest on the team, I would be doing all sorts of odd jobs in the timber mill, because it was timber mill work all up and down the coast. Plus there was all the rural work of corn cutting, pea picking and potato picking and dairy work. For a moment there, I was mechanically minded. I thought I might get an apprenticeship working in a garage, but I was too restless to lock into anything of that nature.[56]

But they had a problem: Jimmy was still of school age and the AWB threatened to send him to Kinchela for not attending classes. Jimmy's grandmother took swift action, enrolling him into St Mary's Catholic School in Moruya, where he would have to catch a bus every day to travel 70 kilometres from Wallaga Lake. He stayed with his Granny Eliza until he was fifteen. He loved living with his Granny Eliza, but did not care too much for the pet magpie she kept, as it followed people around and made itself at home inside the house.

After leaving school, Jimmy was free to travel up and down the coast again, working alongside his dad. Even though he did not do much performing himself those days, Kunkus would try to encourage Jimmy to sing in front of crowds. Once his cousin Peter Brierly taught Jimmy how to play the guitar, there was no stopping him, so Kunkus began taking him to the local talent quests and concerts, and even entering him in contests in Sydney. Kunkus also encouraged Jimmy's brothers and sisters, who remained in Nowra, to sing and perform, and their Aunty Jane prepared them to perform at school concerts and church congregations. It was clear they all had talent, and plenty of mettle, which was no surprise given their vaudevillian parents, and with their Uncle Jack Little urging them on in the background.

Jimmy Little (second from left), aged 16, at the Nowra School of Arts Talent Quest, 1953.

It was my dad who was always my mentor and the most
supportive member of the family. He bought me my
first guitar, and he was the one who helped to arrange
my audition on *Amateur Hour*. And he's the one who
walked around Sydney, around Darling Harbour, before
it was Darling Harbour, waiting with me for the audition
appointment time, in York Street – and we barely had
a quince to share. That's how poor the money was those
days, and how big my dad's heart was. Spending his last
penny on dressing me up, getting a guitar and making the
arrangements, with the help of some of his friends, for the
appointments and so on.[57]

Even though Kunkus and his brother Jack no longer did much touring and performing in those days, they had already built quite a reputation on the South Coast during the 1930s after leaving the Wallaga Lake Gum Leaf Band and forming the Leaf Band. This new band had gained popularity and reviews all up and down the coast. One such review described one of their performances in the local newspapers in Ulladulla as 'a razzamatazz'.

> The audience would be whipped up to excitement pitch
> during the show. Then the sessions would close with the
> song 'The Battlefields of Europe' [correct title 'Break the
> News to Mother', 1897]. The chorus line 'Tell mother not
> to wait for me, for I'm not coming home' would always
> make the audience crumble. That is why the cast made it
> a practice to pass out paper handkerchiefs to the audience
> as they went into the hall.

The troupe's instrumentalists played leaves, jewsharps, harmonicas and violins to create 'a fair razzamatazz'. This is a colloquial description of a 1920s jazz style incorporating 'novelty noise' effects such as growls, waawaas and wails, a factor that arguably popularised gumleaf playing at the time. The Little brothers' 'corroboree' contributions (traditional dances with sticks and spears) were influenced by the lively musical tradition developed further south at their home base of Wallaga Lake.[58]

Jimmy was close to his Uncle Jack, who could no longer perform due to illness, and remembered with deep sadness the day he died.

In his last days, he had sugar diabetes and his body would be full of aches and pains. I used to get methylated spirits in a bottle and massage my Uncle Jack's legs and shoulders and arms to ease the pain as best I could. Because I didn't know what was going on – I just knew Uncle Jack was sick – and he asked me, 'Son, would you rub me here and rub me there with that metho?', I gladly did it, because I didn't want to see my uncle in pain. I did that for quite some time, you know, from day to day, different days.

Then I remember us going to the hospital with Uncle Bill Brierley. Uncle Jack was in a coma behind the screen. I'd never seen anybody that sick before. I was looking at Uncle Jack, the one I tried to help feel better, breathing his last, and it was a matter of hours before he passed away. Uncle Bill broke down and he walked out, and I walked out with him.

A few days later we were on the back of the truck going to Wallaga Lake to the cemetery for his burial. I had my boyhood memories of my dad and Uncle Jack singing on stage, thrilling the audiences wherever they went. To have those kind of memories and see that kind of ending was quite a lot to take in as a kid.

Jimmy suspected that Kunkus's musical gift came from his father, Jimmy's grandfather, John Little senior, whom he vaguely remembered from a photograph as a very tall man with a bushy beard, holding a violin. The story of Jimmy's grandfather is a mysterious one. During an interview in 1965, Kunkus was recorded as saying his father, John Edward Little, was probably born around 1875, in an Aboriginal camp in Queensland, but was raised by Whites in Charleville.[59] John was little more than a toddler when the Aboriginal camp he lived in was set upon by a group of intruders, who massacred the adults there and kidnapped the children,[60] then distributed them out to White families. This was oral family history passed down to him by his father John; however, stories like these have become easier to believe in the last decade or so, as several scholars have been able to establish that this was the usual practice of the Queensland Native Mounted Police during that era.[61]

Kunkus told Jimmy that his father was found hiding in a hollow log when he was captured. Then he was raised (forced to work is a more accurate description) by that White family, who gave him the English name of John Edward Little. John grew up learning to play the violin and apparently 'spoke very good English'. When he was old enough, he escaped from Queensland and went to live in New South Wales, to avoid living under the repressive colonial laws of the state of his birth;[62] this too was not unusual. With conflicting details on his death and marriage certificates, it is thought that John may have lived in Bourke, New

South Wales, for a time, but he was later found to be living at Warangesda Mission near Darlington Point, where, in 1896, he married a woman by the name of Julia Cubby who was with child; however, she and the child died that same year. The New South Wales police salary records indicate that by 1899 John Little was working at Emu Flat, not far from Braidwood in New South Wales. This is where he most likely met his second wife Eliza Brierley, marrying her in 1902 at Wallaga Lake.

By the time he arrived at Braidwood, John Little was a highly accomplished tracker, having been employed by the Emu Flat Police Station from 1899 until 1902 as a replacement for the locally renowned tracker John Alick Bond, who was away fighting in the Boer War. Remarkably skilled in their craft, a tracker in those days not only had the responsibility to track down bushrangers, many of whom flocked to the areas of Captains Flat, Araluen and Braidwood because they were gold and silver mining towns; they also looked for people who were lost or suspected dead, as well as finding missing stock.

Further records establish that in 1900 John Little was called away on a search for the famous bushranger Jimmy Governor,[63] whom most people know as Jimmie Blacksmith, the man whom the film *The Chant of Jimmie Blacksmith* is named after. Although the New South Wales police had called upon the Native Police Force, a team of trackers from Queensland, to assist them in this search, John was also called up from Braidwood, arriving in the Manning Valley on 27 September. Within a month, Jimmy Governor was finally captured, on 27 October. With his services no longer needed, John was sent back to the Southern Tablelands of New South Wales on the 28 October. However good John's reputation as a tracker may have been, when Kunkus told him that his grandfather John Little was one of the best, Jimmy could only speculate that this was indeed the case. Proud of his father John's warrior spirit and Queensland heritage, Kunkus would write a song about his father, calling it the 'Queensland Song'.[64]

> *Well my father he was Black*
> *And the Whiteman called him Jack*
> *So remember we are still Abos*
> *Fighting for what we adore*
> *Peace, goodwill for evermore*
> *For remember we are still Abos*
> *Will we fight them with our boomerangs, our nullas and our spears*
> *Oh remember the war cry*
> *Oh the Abo will be there*
> *Think of our fathers they were brave*
> *And their sons were just the same*
> *For remember we are Abos*

Jimmy's grandfather died in 1932, before he was born, but like his father Kunkus, Jimmy wrote a song in his honour, although, in the song, he does not specify where John did his tracking. He called it 'Black Tracker'. Jimmy would have success with the song, recording it with two of his Aboriginal contemporaries, Col Hardy and Roger Knox. The song continues to speak to many Aboriginal families who are proud of their tracker ancestors.

> *You know about Glenrowan coz you had a job to do*
> *You know about Uralla, you were needed up there too*
> *You mounted with the troopers in their uniform of blue*

> *Hmm, Black Tracker I am proud of you*
> *Coz no-one else could tell if someone passed this way you see*
> *No rugged land or desert sand could hide the mystery*
> *So warrior my brother, I am forever proud of you*
> *Hmm, Black Tracker I am proud of you*
> *Though your name is seldom mentioned*
> *Your art is never slack*
> *Walked proud and tall amongst them all you gentleman of black*
> *Coz no-one loves this country any better than you do*
> *Hmm, Black Tracker I am proud of you*
> *And they still need you.*

Kunkus himself would die on 28 March 1972 at the age of sixty-one, after contracting bronchitis, and being hospitalised in Bega. He had been living in a timber hut in Nerrigundah, alongside the Tuross River, not too far from Wallaga Lake, as a semi-recluse suffering with asthma, and was frequently cared for by his long-time partner, Dora Williams. The night before he died, Kunkus spoke to Jimmy on the phone – who by then had been living in Sydney for many years – and asked if Jimmy could come down to Bega to take him out of hospital, but Jimmy had not realised that his father was dying, and thought his dad was in the best of care. He was not to know that his father was asking Jimmy not to let him die in hospital.

> He rang me from the hospital in Bega. I was in Sydney, and I could hear him, you know, gasping for breath. And I said, 'Well, you're in hospital, Dad.' And I wanted to speak to the nursing sisters and [ask], you know, 'What's happening with my dad?'

And next day he passed away. And I, he just, he wanted me to come and get him. 'Son, come and get me out of hospital and take me home.' I said, 'Dad, you're in the right place, in hospital. I'll come down as soon as I can and see you in hospital.'[65]

One of the musical gifts that Kunkus left behind was the only remaining recording of the original members of the Wallaga Lake Gum Leaf Band. Another important legacy was that he penned the lyrics to a song that Jimmy recorded for the record label Regal Zonophone in 1958. It was probably the first ever Aboriginal protest song to be recorded for commercial purposes and was about Aboriginal people denied employment on the basis of their race. Kunkus's song is called 'Give the Coloured Lad a Chance'.[66]

Well, my name is Jimmy Little
And from Wallaga Lake I came
A lovely little spot along the coast
With mountains and the hills
Lovely lakes and rippling dells
That make the sweetest music all the day
I went to the city
Trying hard to find some work
I travelled the city night and day
I went to place to place
With starvation on my face
But the people say no coloureds they employ
I'm an honest Koori lad
And to work I'm not afraid

To please you, I'd rather sing or dance
I'd do anything you'd say
If you only name the day
If you'd only give us coloured lads a chance.

Before he died, Kunkus was able to see his son achieve national fame, and record the song he wrote. It also moved him to see his children Freddy, Betty, Colin and Monica appear on the stage and television. It gave him bragging rights, which he never held back on. Kunkus would live long enough to see his son Freddy branch off and take up with a musical career of his own, appearing regularly on the stage at the Auburn RSL Club for many years, until he died in 1987. His other son, Jimmy's brother, Colin, also sang at local events around Nowra, where he stayed with his Aunty Jane until he moved in with his partner, Jenny Parsons, in Braidwood during the 1980s. Jimmy's two sisters were also singers. Monica, who was considered to be the one with the most beautiful voice in the Little family, sang at various events on the South Coast and western Sydney, around Doonside, where she lived for many years before moving to Newcastle in the 1990s. Monica's second eldest daughter, Deborah Cheetham, would become Australia's first Aboriginal sopranist and the writer and director of two operas: *Pecan Summer* (2010) and *Eumeralla, A War Requiem for Peace* (2018). Betty also sang, sometimes taking her son Tony on the stage with her, but mostly she entertained as a busker and educated others about the political hardship and sexual abuse that she and other Aboriginal women endured. Betty also appeared briefly in a feature film called *Jindalee Lady*, in 1992; it was directed by Brian Syron and produced by Brianne Kearney.

Jimmy Little Snr. (centre) with Arthur McLeod (left) and Margaret Williams (right) performing for NAIDOC in Martin Place, Sydney, 1961.

There were times when Kunkus's children performed on the stage with each other or occasionally together as a family, but only in an informal way, and there were also times when Jimmy shared the stage with his father Kunkus. One such occasion, when Jimmy was booked to appear at an event which took place in July 1961, Jimmy invited Kunkus to play his gumleaf to the crowd on the National Aboriginal Observance Day in Martin Place, in front of government dignitaries. A long and proud family tradition – from John Little (1875–1932) to Kunkus (1911–1972) to his son Jimmy (1937–2012) and Jimmy's daughter Frances Little (1958–) and her son James Henry Little (1979–) – the gift of music continues in the Little family.

CHAPTER 5

'Life is like a Lottery'

The high-tech world of business
Can be taxing on the mind
It's a tough side of life we all endure,
And the pioneering spirit
We all seem to possess
Keeps us ever going forward to explore

Every kind of business
Be it big or be it small
Has its pressure and pleasure that's for sure,
And to keep on surviving
All the trauma there within
We need therapeutic medicated cure

We all try to relax
With self-given time
For the more important things we adore,
Travelling in the fast lane
Doesn't always spell success
It depends on what you're out there looking for

Frances Peters-Little

Good health in mind and body
Is the best guarantee
You'll deal with whatever lays in store,
Most people like a challenge
To test their mental grit
It's a general well-accepted kind of law

At the end of the day
What we do and what we say
Is our life to be safe and secure,
The world is full of good
With an equal share of bad
It's difficult to detect every flaw

In this modern world we live
We take and we give
Like taking chances in a game of drawing straws,
We exist in a system
With little room for change
And we cop the lot squarely on the jaw

Then start putting things together
In our daily picture frame
Like a puzzle party game of jigsaw,
Life is like a lottery
Taking chances on the trot
Even though there's so much out there to deplore,
Pride, good character and fairness

Will enable us to win
Our deserving lucky first prize at the door.

On the day Jimmy finally left the South Coast, he was sixteen years old, and he left in an old Bob Lavis truck that regularly delivered fresh produce to Sydney markets. Although he had travelled this way with his dad many times before, this time he set out alone, encouraged by Kunkus and another musician friend by the name of Pat Ware, who arranged for him to stay temporarily with a family called the Clarks.

I had a little port, a few things, and my arrangements were made to arrive at this house on the Princes Highway in Sylvania Heights. The night before, after bean picking, the truck was loaded up and I bid farewell to Aunty Jane, Dad and all the kids. The truck was loaded with beans – bags and bags of beans – and it would journey from there just after dinner at night, late in the evening, whatever, and it would slowly wind its way up to Sydney and get in to the markets first thing in the morning and offload its produce. I remember climbing up on top of the load of beans and sitting right in the middle, on the truck, way up top, travelling all evening till early morning until I arrived at Sylvania Heights.

When they pulled up at the house where I was going to get off, I thanked the driver and went around the back of the house and sat on the porch there, and went to sleep sitting in the chair waiting for the Clark family to wake up. Eventually, Margie Clark walked out the veranda and saw me there, and seemed really pleased to see me.

Jimmy Little and Pat Ware, 1956.

Pat Ware was an English-born, gun-picking guitar player who lived in Berrima, a little town in the Southern Highlands not far from the South Coast. Pat already had a reputation for being one of Sydney's most popular studio session guitarists, with Regal Zonophone. He had heard Jimmy's audition on *Australia's Amateur Hour*, watched him perform at a few shows down the South Coast, and had taken an instant liking to the young singer.[67]

The Amateur Hour program was a national talent quest show broadcast through 2GB [and later 2UE and 2UW] Australia-wide. I used to listen to the show at home when I was going to school and it was then compered by Dick Fair – Dick Fair's national Amateur Hour. By the time I got my audition to do Dick Fair's Amateur Hour, it was Terry Dear who took over the program. I was successful enough to get second place on the bill. I was narrowly beaten by a trained tenor on the night, who took out the honours. But there were ten contestants and I was number two. Even Chad Morgan appeared on the same program as me, and he continues his career today from early radio.

In its heyday, the *Australia's Amateur Hour* program toured to several locations across Australia seeking out exciting new talent, but it was almost at the end of its era by the time Jimmy auditioned. The program took a serious approach to finding anyone who might have a burning desire to pursue a career in the entertainment industry. In many regards it was similar to Australia's popular television program *Australian Idol*.[68] Regardless of its successful run of eighteen years from 1940 to 1958, it was unable to compete with television, which came to Australia in 1957.

Radio had a huge impact on Jimmy's life. Commercial radio first broadcast in Australia in 1923 on 2SB (Broadcasters Sydney Limited).[69] The 1940s and 1950s became the golden years of radio,[70] and by 1947 more than 40 per cent of Australians preferred radio, while only 27 per cent wanted to read. By the 1950s more than 80 per cent of radio listeners were listening in to commercial radio,[71] and Jimmy's earliest influences from radio were American artists such as Guy Mitchell, Eddie Fisher, Al Martino, Bing Crosby, Perry Como, Vic Damone and Dick Haymes. He also enjoyed listening to local radio stars such as Tex Morton and Buddy Williams, and a whole lot of others like Smoky Dawson, Tim McNamara, Rick and Thel Carey and Dusty Rankin. It was ironic, according to Jimmy, that Australia's first hillbilly star was New Zealander Tex Morton – Morton arrived in Australia in 1932 touring his 'Australasian sound' and inspiring promising young artists like Buddy Williams and Slim Dusty, whom Jimmy held in high regard, to take up the bush ballad singing lifestyle.

I truly admire a long-time legend who has since passed on, in the name of Slim Dusty. I admire him for his dedication and consistency, in presenting the bush balladeer; [he was] a singer who wrote and sang about the whole of Australia in the storyline of his life, because he never wavered, because he never altered his course. He kept going forward, and at the same time he kept entertaining the public who weren't able to come to his shows. He would take his shows to the community, to the public, who appreciated him to no end. Because he did that constantly, he became a national hero in the eyes of Indigenous Australians and non-Indigenous Australians, because of his Australiana. I admired him and still do, and see him as one of my heroes of the early days when I was growing up and listening to his work.

Jimmy was greatly influenced by hillbilly music on the radio, describing the songs as 'bush ballads and stories of singing songs around the campfire in the days of droving'. Since Jimmy came from the bush he was drawn to songs about shearing, fencing and rural work of all kinds, such as working in the timber yards, dairies and the fisheries. He called them love songs of a sort, whether it was love of country, or nature, as well as romantic love. Hillbilly music, and not country music, was what most Australians sang from the 1920s to the early 1940s. In Jimmy's opinion, country and western music was a modern thing and did not come into its own until the late 1940s–1960s, when radio stars like Reg Lindsay and the McKean Sisters came on the scene.

Jimmy's friend Pat Ware, who was already well known as a hillbilly artist, began working on the Sydney scene with Jimmy in the 1950s. One of the agents they worked for labelled them the 'Continental Duo', probably because Pat was English and Jimmy was Aboriginal. The name stuck until the band expanded to include a bass player, and subsequently, with Jimmy at the helm as their lead singer, the Continental Duo became the Jimmy Little Trio.

Eventually Pat decided maybe we ought to incorporate another member in the band, particularly a bass player that added rhythm. Then we teamed up with – Graham Tredenick was his name – but we called him Nick. He was the double-bass player; Pat was the lead guitarist and I was rhythm guitar. So, for a time, we worked as a trio, and on occasions Graham would play the accordion. So it was interesting how the band started to form and the sound we began to create.

One of the first things Jimmy did when they started performing in Sydney was to buy new clothes and a new guitar. He wanted to seek out the many other talent quests that were around the Sydney music scene at the time. His greatest wish was to get himself a recording contract, and through Pat and Nick he was being introduced to a wide variety of recording artists and local venues around town.

Jimmy's daytime job was working in the timber yards at Mascot. This was work he was familiar with from his time with his father on the South Coast. The daily travel from Sylvania Heights to Mascot began to take its toll on Jimmy, so he eventually left the Clarks and moved to a boarding house in St Peters run by a Mr and Mrs Scott.

In the few months before moving, I would get up early in the morning, at the Clarks' place on the Princes Highway, and get a bus into Hurstville train station and then get a train to Marrickville, and then get another bus from Marrickville out to the timber yard. I would go to work in the morning in the dark, early hours, and come home in the dark. I didn't mind that at first – it was all exciting for me to be doing this as a new kid straight out of the bush and into the city, with commuters hustling and bustling along.

The Scotts had a private home with a few rooms for boarders and that was the fashion, for people to rent out the different rooms for single workers, male and female. So I got a room there and shared it for a while with Jim Ware, Pat's younger brother, in Goodsell

Street. I stayed in touch with the Clarks, and of course Pat was only a suburb away in Marrickville, and we were spending weekends together performing and I was getting to know the industry.

In those days, the places we worked were the town hall concerts and the dances, and the occasional party. Back then, hotels would close at six o'clock in the day – like all shops and businesses. So there was no place to go and have a quiet drink in the lounge, in the bar rooms of hotels anywhere afterwards, because they were all closed. But when the licensing opened for late night trading and afternoon trading, that meant afternoon concerts and Sunday concerts in the beer garden. This was really great for people who wanted to have a quiet drink and a little music and something to eat.

Jimmy did not confine himself to the trio. He also enjoyed working as a solo artist, performing for many of the Aboriginal dances held in Redfern and La Perouse back in the 1950s. He also performed on the *Kalang* showboat, which allowed him to be flexible in his music and play for a broader audience. The *Kalang* showboat was a large Sydney ferry converted into an auditorium that sailed on Sydney Harbour for the enormously popular country music concert cruises.

One of my favourite shows to appear in was a ferry on the harbour. It was, I think, once a month, or maybe once every two weeks, on a Wednesday or a Tuesday night. All the known country artists and the yet-to-be-known artists would appear at this concert. It was two hours of eats and drinks and concert on the harbour of Sydney on the old ferry called *Kalang*. It was very popular, and I loved it. So, I would sing the most modern up-to-date country songs as well as the old-time traditionals. It was a matter of sussing out the audience, who was there, and who was on the show with you. I would always work my repertoire and program around my fellow artists, and around the audiences. If the audience was mostly my generation, well, then I'd sing songs that they would know. If they were an older generation, then I would sing songs that would match their mood and their style of listening. So it was fun to be able to sing to mixed audiences in a theme that was appropriate at the time. However, most of my showboat shows were broadly country music. But my repertoire for the hotels and nightclubs – I'd sing evergreen classics and ballads. Other times I'd sing pop songs, dance music or rockabilly at the town halls. It was a great time, the whole experience of all these venues. Some I did with a band, others I did alone, but it all helped me to become versatile.

Throughout this time, Jimmy kept his sights on getting a recording contract. His first audition was with Regal Zonophone, which later became EMI,[72] and which had already signed Pat and Nicky.

Pat and I went there, and we had an audition with Ron Wills, the then directing manager. He said to me and Pat that he liked what he could hear from me, and he said, 'What we'd like now is for you to come back in a few months' time with some of your own songs, because we're keen to record overseas songs on the A side and Australian songs on the B side of the single recording'. So that prompted Pat and I to get into song writing, so we could record our own material on the flip side of these recordings. In all we went back something like five, six months later, and Mr Wills said, 'Fine,' so he signed us up straightaway there and then, and we made our first record together.

During their time with Regal Zonophone, Pat dealt with the business side of their relationship and Jimmy concentrated on the music. Jimmy and Pat would record about three to four singles a year, Jimmy's first recording being in 1956, when he sang Kitty Well's song 'The Heartbreak Waltz' on the A side, and Jean Shepard's 'Mysteries of Life' on the flip side. All in all, Jimmy recorded sixteen tracks with Regal Zonophone; including 'Someday You're Gonna Call Me', 'Stolen Moments', 'Sweet Mama', 'A Fool Such As I', 'It's Time To Pay', 'My Foot Is On The Stair', 'The Grandest Show of All', 'Golden Wrist Watch', 'Why Must There Be A Tomorrow?', 'Silver City Comet', 'Frances Claire', 'Waiting For You', 'The Coloured Lad' and 'Oh! Lonely Heart'. Pat and Jimmy wrote several songs together, but the songs he recorded solo were 'Frances Claire', which he wrote about his then eighteen-week-old daughter and his father's song, 'The Coloured Lad'.

With his radio and recording success, his musical appearances began to include work outside Sydney, at places like Picton, Camden, Campbelltown, Lithgow, Bowral, Mittagong, Katoomba, Gosford and Wollongong. Without cars, Jimmy, Pat and double-bass player Nick relied on being able to catch trains to all their venues. Those places weren't really far from Sydney, but with train as their only method of transport, they seemed a long distance away. All three of them had 'day jobs', so it made little sense for them to travel any further than these New South Wales towns.

Pat and I played for a good number of years, until he became a family man, and he was also still 'day-working'. He had four children – three girls and a boy – and he and his wife, Joy, decided to raise the family up in the country, and they went up to Tamworth. So I continued on making a few changes with my band members, to keep the Jimmy Little Trio thing happening. Pat and I had an amicable departure. We never had any kind of disagreements of any sort. We just saw that the two paths were going to go separate ways and wished each other well.

Pat's leaving added to various reasons that Jimmy had for ending his contract with Regal Zonophone. By this time, Jimmy craved the opportunity to expand his musical repertoire from hillbilly music to more pop tunes, which was something he appreciated from his days performing on the *Kalang*. He also became very interested in being a part of a new exciting Australian recording company at the time, Festival Records.[73]

I wasn't strictly a country artist back then. I had the freedom to sing all kinds of songs that I was doing live. That's the reason why I joined Festival Records. They gave me this wide scope of material to sing, whereas Regal Zonophone wanted to label me as just a hillbilly country singer. That was fine, I could've stayed with them for a long time, but I was limiting my career. Festival Records gave me this new broad freedom to do everything, which I did.

By 1959 there was no shortage of singing jobs for Jimmy, who had now left his day job at the Mascot timber yards and taken one at Dri Glo towels in Homebush. He had also been offered a major role in a Hollywood feature film called *Shadow of the Boomerang*.[74] When he accepted this opportunity to appear in a film, Jimmy left Sydney and headed to the shooting location on a property near Moree in north-west New South Wales. It was there that he declared he had finally 'thrown in the towel' on all his daytime jobs.

Jimmy was also finding less time to head down to the South Coast, to be with his father and siblings.

I didn't get back much to the South Coast, because I was in a loop that meant a certain amount of time and energy and commitment, so my little visits away from the city back home were just enough to let everyone know that I was not gone for good or forever or that I hadn't forgotten my roots. The people back home – relatives and friends – in the main, most of them were quite happy with my success, such as they saw it, and they didn't seem to think that I changed all that much. They could see that I was now a Sydneysider; but once I spent some time with them, they realised that I hadn't changed completely, I was just the same old me on the inside, maybe a little different on the outside, but on the inside was the same old me.

Jimmy would receive some criticisms for not spending more time with his South Coast community, even though he had just turned twenty-two and was in demand workwise; by this time he had also married his sweetheart, Marjorie Rose, and had become a father to their first child, Frances, in 1958. In other words, he was only doing what his father encouraged him to do, and that was to follow his dreams and grasp at opportunities, just as Kunkus himself had done.

I had to live my life and I couldn't live their way, so it was getting on with the job of finding out more about myself and my desire to succeed in the way that I did. So, I just kept going.

After Jimmy signed with Festival Records in 1959, he was soon enjoying early chart success on radio with the Irish ballad 'Danny Boy', written by Frederic Weatherly in 1913. Jimmy's version of 'Danny Boy' peaked at number nine on Sydney radio in 1959, with 'This Lucky Old Sun' on the B side. Then, in February 1960, his next single, 'El Paso', reached number six on the charts in Adelaide and number twelve in Sydney, and included 'The Last Rose of Summer' on the B side.[75] 'El Paso' is a country and western ballad written and originally recorded by Marty Robbins, whom Jimmy was later very glad to meet and perform with at the Mooroopna Country Music festival, in 1976.

As Jimmy expanded his music career, the music scene in Sydney began to boom. No longer limited to hillbilly musical shows, recordings and performances, a completely new world of musical variety and events was opening up. It was as if anything was possible, which urged him on to become more versatile in his own performances, as was only natural for someone who had grown up in a vaudevillian family.

The jazz scene was happening; the blues scene was happening. There were the comedy theatres; there was the variety of dance and orchestral, old-time music. There was a whole range of things that were happening that I previously didn't do, only because I was limited to this one stream of country music. But as I broadened my repertoire, including other kinds of music other than just country, then I became a participant in other shows. So, the big dances, the radio shows, the big concert halls and nightclubs, as we know them today, the suburban nightclubs, the football clubs, the RSL clubs, the bowling clubs, golf, tennis, you name it. I was on the threshold of a whole new industry that was about to bloom and blossom across the nation.

With the clubs and television developing, you got more variety artists coming into the picture, so I ended up working within the club scene, with jugglers – like side acts, they call them. Magicians, comics and fire-eaters, and jugglers and bike riders and all the kind of acts you see in circuses. They were refined and entertaining – ventriloquists, acts with a guillotine, and male and female performers. The bands would be resident bands of four and five pieces. It was very sophisticated, really, when I moved into the scene in a much more diverse way. But I still maintained my country audience by occasionally working the country scene, and [I would go] across the border into the jazz and blues scene and the old-time scene of golden oldies and things.

Now that he was part of Festival Records, Jimmy began meeting new artists who relied on commercial radio. 2SM radio (St Mary's) catered to country music audiences, and Jimmy became a part of the team of artists who were 2SM regulars. There, he would find other artists who became his contemporaries, and it was also where he met his long-time manager, Ted Quigg.

Ted Quigg arranged to have a thirty-minute country 'hour' called *On The Trail*, on 2SM in the heart of Sydney. All the urban cowboys and cowgirls were living in Sydney, like Alan Hirst, Nola

Hirst, Judy Stone, Lonnie Lee was one of them, and the brothers from Queensland – the Webb brothers – and Frank Ifield, who was already very popular. Other well-known country artists were on the road, like Slim Dusty, Smoky Dawson, Reg Lindsay and many others. They had some radio shows, but they constantly had to travel, selling their records on tour. They weren't city-based, like I was, so I had become like a city cowboy who stayed behind and 'toured the city', so to speak, from suburb to suburb, from town hall to town hall, and radio station to radio station.

With television becoming more popular, people like Smoky Dawson, who had his own television show in the United States of America, and Reg Lindsay, who had a country music television show that lasted more than twelve years, caused music shows to reach incredible ratings. Reg Lindsay's program, which incidentally won more than one TV Week Logie award, was able to showcase a range of Australian singers, including Jimmy and several other Aboriginal performers, such as Auriel Andrew[76] and Colin Hardy.[77]

Jimmy appeared on television both before and after his national hit 'Royal Telephone', which was recorded in 1963 and became a hit in 1964. His first appearance was on *Bandstand* – an Australian live variety pop music television program which screened from November 1958 to June 1972. It featured both local and international music artists, was produced in-house at the studios of TCN-9 in Willoughby, New South Wales, and was hosted by Brian Henderson. Running concurrently was Australian rock idol Johnny O'Keefe's show, *Six O'Clock Rock*, the ABC's Saturday evening teenage music show, which ran from 1959 to 1962, on which Jimmy was a regular feature. Both country and pop artists were appearing on television and Jimmy was lucky to be able to straddle both genres and take advantage of the new opportunities provided by the medium.

When television happened, that put a face to the voice and to the name of people on radio. It just got bigger and better. Then there was a whole heap of new artists who weren't country artists. They were called pop artists, by the names of Johnny O'Keefe, Col Joye, Johnny Devlin, Jay Justin, Warren Williams, Dave Bridge Band. And the girls were Judy Stone, Patsy Ann Nobel, Noelene Batley. And a whole heap of performers came through with the television and recordings as well. So here I was in two kinds of music, developing two kinds of styles, and being a dual artist performing in all these venues. When I would do a country show, I'd be with all the country artists that I knew, and when I did a pop show, I'd be with the pop artists, growing up and treading the boards with them.

CHAPTER 6

'Waterloo Town Hall'

We met one night just briefly
At a-dancehall in old 'Waterloo'
My attention she captured completely
Like nobody else could do
Gracefully dancing here in my arms
In a-magical moment of bliss
Charming, delightful and cheery
With a-smile I just couldn't resist

Enquiring if I would be singing
If so, could she make a request
'Rose-Marie' was then selected
I sang it at my very best
We waltzed to an old-time barn-dance
As rotation partners would change
When the musical set was over
Her sweetness within me remained

200+ happy young people
Merrily took to the floor

Frances Peters-Little

Inspiring/admiring each other
Right-up to the final encore
Pretty-girls in beautiful dresses
And handsome good-looking young dudes
All wanting to make an impression
On the person they likely would choose

But me I felt like a-misfit
With my dial and long, lanky frame
In my boots this quiet country-cowboy
In this big city slickers' domain
Then all too soon it was over
As friends all gathered for home
In buses, trains and taxis
While some of us walked home alone

Then one night I finally got lucky
I escorted (4) friends to their door
Each lady was nice and thanked me
And I never had done that before
But the last girl I said good night to
Had already stolen my heart
I needed her name and her number
Cause I loved her right from the start

Since then, we both began dating
Boyfriend, girlfriend were we
We took in the sights of the city
So happy-go-lucky and free

> *Three years of court-ship commitment*
> *A foundation of friendship and fun*
> *A-honeymoon/wedding together*
> *Two hearts ever beating as one.*

Jimmy was seventeen when he met Marjorie Rose Peters, at an Aboriginal football fundraising dance at Waterloo Town Hall and, as the song suggests, he was clearly smitten from that moment. Marj later described him as a flashy young man who rode a bicycle, wearing bright Presley purple socks everywhere. In spite of Marj appearing somewhat aloof, Jimmy persisted in trying to win her heart. He succeeded, because after several weeks of friendship, they began dating. The rest, as they say, is history, and their marriage would become known as one of the most respected ones in the Australian music industry.[78] Even fifty-three years after they met, on their Golden Wedding anniversary, Jimmy still delighted in telling the story of their meeting, in vivid detail.

It was during a barn dance when we'd met. She saw that I had a guitar and she said, 'Are you going to sing? Are you a singer?', and I said, 'Yeah, I'm going to try; if I get a chance, I'll sing,' and she put a request in. During the few moments we were dancing, she said, 'Would you sing "Rose Marie" for me?' It was popular at the time and I knew the words and I said, 'Yeah, I might,' but I was just trying to sound cool – then it was time to change partners. But I did notice Marj more so than anybody else. I mean, when you're young you go into a crowded room of people of your own age and you like them all, but if somebody stands out, well, in the case of Marj, she's the one that stood out, maybe because she requested the song, and was the only one who requested the song, and I wanted to dance some more with her. We got along well right from the beginning.

After a few more dances, like weekend to weekend, I got her phone number and asked her to go out to the pictures, to the movies, and she said yes. So, we became steady boy- and girlfriend over a matter of weeks. But there was a time when I escorted all the girls home. The girls would get about in little groups of company, like four or five girls would travel on the train, or travel in a taxi, or walk. It was like that, the boys would be in little groups and the girls would be in little groups, and whenever a pair would pair up, then they would go off together. But Marj was going home to her job, like the other girls, Junie Holten, Hazel Bolt, Jenny Dodd and Audrey Welsh, and Marj. I remember they were waiting for a cab outside the dance; the cabs would come by and pick everybody up and, I don't know, I just wanted to accompany them all home. In those days you could fit more people in the cab than today, there used to be two in the front with the driver and three in the back, and sometimes four. So, whatever the case was then, all the girls and I just got in the cab and we were dropped off, for each girl at their respective place where they worked, and this is around Woollahra and Vaucluse and in that general area, like Paddington. So, everybody got off, one at a time, and I stayed with the cab, and I was waiting with Marj. Marj got to her destination and got out and I was too shy to get out with her, and I bid her goodnight and went home in the cab myself. Later on, or the next day actually, all the girls rang Marj to see what happened with Jimmy, and she said he was too shy to get out of the cab, something to that effect, but we were going to go out to the pictures one day.

So I think probably that happened with a lot of the young people in those days, escorting others home and trying to get better acquainted with one or the other. But I never lost my attraction for Marj all the way through and whenever we met at singalongs at my friend Claude Williams's family's place in Surry Hills, I was always on the lookout for her, and I like to think that she was also waiting to see me.

Marj had only arrived in Sydney a few months before Jimmy and had taken up work as a live-in domestic servant in Vaucluse – at this time, during the 1950s, the Australian Government was enacting its policy to assimilate Aboriginal people into White society.[79]

Both Jimmy and Marj were the eldest children in their respective families,[80] and they considered their move to Sydney as merely an opportunity to find work and to help their families back home. Even though Marj's family did not make financial demands upon her,[81] she thought that she might be able to help them by being financially independent and by 'testing the waters' of big city life for her younger brothers and sisters. Jimmy, on the other hand, came to Sydney to work and sent back what money he could afford to his Aunty Jane, who at that stage was raising Betty, Monica and Colin. The girls were still of school age, but later, when they left school, Aunty Jane sent Betty to an Aborigines Inland Mission Bible Training College near Singleton, New South Wales, where she took to Christianity for a while and became a nurse. Monica, on the other hand, rebelled against the heavy-handed Christian life that Aunty Jane encouraged her to embrace. 'Aunty Jane always

Jimmy and Marj, Redfern, 1957.

kept a big houseful of people at her place. She was known as everyone's mother.'[82]

So there were a lot of people who depended upon her. It was great that she was also able to take my two sisters under her care, on top of all those other people, and so I felt I needed to send money back to my Aunty Jane. So did my dad, who was still working, and my brothers Freddy and Colin, who had jobs by now. I would have liked to have sent more money back for my sisters, but the reality was that even though Marj and I were 'doing alright' in the city, us Aboriginal people living in the city were still making less than everyone else and getting jobs at the bottom rung of the ladder compared to Whites.

By the time Jimmy and Marj arrived in Sydney, the policy of assimilation was at its peak. While much has been spoken about the negative effects of assimilation on their generation, a great many Aboriginal people saw the government's ambitions for them as a great opportunity to help them break away from the hardships and restraints of 'mission life' and gain a better future for themselves.

In Jimmy's case, assimilation was something he neither rejected nor embraced. If the truth be known, he had not even given it much thought. It had not occurred to him or Marj that the policies of assimilation meant that they would have to forgo their pride in their Aboriginality or forget where they came from and deny their family ties, even if that had been the government's intention. Jimmy and Marj both grew up witnessing their parents' struggle against the hardships of mission life and the laws of segregation, and they considered the policy of assimilation a softer option. To their credit, Jimmy and Marj, like so many young Aboriginal people at that time, were able to withstand a hefty assault of political and social pressure to 'be more like Whites', and only thought of themselves as 'modern Aboriginal people'.

Neither of them felt a need to express their personal objections towards the policy of assimilation by taking to the streets or using other means of political action. Instead, they kept their feelings private. In the years that followed, though, younger generations of Aboriginal people expressed their anger over the assimilation policies, and while Jimmy saw the importance of their actions, he did not engage in such activities himself. However, he occasionally spoke out when he was questioned by the media. Even when Jimmy and the many Aboriginal people of his generation who came to Sydney to 'make a go' of life were criticised, they just persevered, while still holding on to their identities.

It was a different generation and a different world for those people, many of whom lived in what Jimmy referred to as 'urban tribes'.

My experiences about our people living before the heady days of the 1960s into the 1970s and beyond are that we lived in fairly close-knit communities, particularly in Redfern and La Perouse, which were thought of as the two suburban missions and meeting places. For me, I had thought of the Redfern and outer areas of Erskineville, St Peters, Glebe and all of that particular area, Alexandria, as places where mostly northerners, where Gooris lived. Gooris came from places as far as Kempsey and beyond Nambucca Heads, Grafton. All the north coasters would come to the Redfern big urban mission, with a sprinkling of the westerners from the north to the south, like Walgett, Moree, Armidale, Bourke, Wellington, Cowra and Griffiths, etc. So, you got a whole bunch of young people coming to town to work, for a career, and they would come and congregate in Redfern, Alexandria, at the various football dances or functions that were on the weekends. And then the southerners who came from Nowra and Bega, all the South Coast area, they would go to La Perouse. So we had these two missions, if you like, that were a mixture of all the westerners, all the northerners and all the southerners.

There were a lot of clashes here and there, but when I say clash, it was not so much a viscous kind of clash, but it was a tribal, a very modern urban tribal mix. I mean the young men – the young men weren't allowed to be friendly with the young ladies from up north, if they were from the south, and vice versa. And the westerners were like the referees; they would come down and they would keep the peace between the north and the south. So if you can think of that influx of young people coming into Sydney, in search of work, careers, and opportunities of all sorts, there was a lovely, lovely mix going on. But there was also an undercurrent of: we can't get along because we had different attitudes, and so we were very different from one another; so the southerners would stay close to the westerners, and the northerners would stay close to the westerners, as a wonderful mix. And that's how I met my wife, who was a Yuwaalaraay/Gamilaraay woman from the west, and me a Yorta Yorta/Yuin-Monaro man from the south.

Before moving to Sydney, Jimmy had heard about two Aboriginal teams that played in the Rugby League second division, and he looked forward to seeing them in action. These two teams were the Redfern All Blacks and the La Perouse All Blacks. When Jimmy met Marj at the dance in the Waterloo Town Hall, it had been a fundraiser for the Redfern All Blacks. The first eye-opener Jimmy had to the urban tribalism that existed in Sydney was through the alliance of Rugby League teams. This 'tribalism' still exists today, as explained by historian Heidi Norman, who suggested that the Koori Football Knockout is perhaps just a modern-day 'corroboree'.

> The football carnival can be understood as a modern and adapted medium for cultural performance and expression, for kinship-based modes of organisation merged with state shaped communities, and for courtship and competition. The football is reminiscent of a four-day traditional ceremonial dance and celebration, but it also enables new social and cultural practices to emerge. It is an opportunity for families to gather, reunite as a community and barrack for their hometown and mob, and commemorate past glories and those who have passed on. The Knockout is fiercely contested; world class, tough football is on display.[83]

When Jimmy and Marj, along with other young Aboriginal people, moved to Sydney in the 1950s, they found themselves mingling with new immigrants who appeared to have the same family values as they did. But, as Jimmy saw it, they were still competing with Aboriginal people for the same jobs and accommodation in the inner city, and they seemed to be able to 'make do'. While it appeared there was plenty of work to go around, for Jimmy it seemed that the immigrants (particularly the British ones) who got the jobs first were more easily accepted and that his people always remained on the bottom rung of the ladder.

The inner-city suburb of Redfern was popular because of its proximity to the country trains terminus, to factories and to cheap housing.[84] La Perouse was originally an Aboriginal camping ground during early settlement and was gazetted by the government in 1895 as an Aboriginal reserve, so it easily became a meeting place for people arriving from the South Coast.[85] Even though Jimmy hailed from that part of New South Wales, he did not stay in La Perouse and moved more around the inner city of Sydney where a lot of other Aboriginal people his age lived.

Well, there was a few of the men who worked with me at the timber yards at Mascot when I was there who were from Kempsey and Nambucca Heads and the South Coast. Then I recall Jim Stanley from Wellington, who had introduced me to Noel Stanley, who also had a beautiful singing voice and joined me some time later in the *[All] Coloured Show*.[86] So, while I had the good company of these new-found non-Aboriginal musical friends from Sylvania Heights, it was great to connect with other Aboriginal friends and family that were spread out across the inner city.

As far as all of the single Aboriginal women I knew, most of them seemed to live and work in the eastern suburbs. Either they were domestic servants, or they worked in the factories like W.D. & H.O. Wills in Kensington, or Sweetacres confectionary down in Rosebery; or they worked over in Unilever's Lever Brothers factories in Balmain. But, at least on the weekends, we'd all get together and go and watch the football, and go to the dances at Waterloo Town Hall, or us men would watch a lot of Aboriginal boxers on

Monday nights, where there were training gyms around Newtown, St Peters and Chippendale. All the women, however, like Marj and her friends, weren't into boxing all that much, but all seemed to be into wrestling. In fact, at one of the places Marj worked at in Rushcutters Bay, a lot of famous wrestlers, like Chief Little Wolf, would stay there and give the girls free tickets to go and see the show at the old Sydney Stadium.

Prior to beginning work in Rushcutters Bay, Marj's work in Vaucluse was as a domestic cleaner and cook for the Harp family, in Hopetoun Avenue. The job had been pre-arranged by the AWB, which also lined up jobs for Marj's sisters Elaine and Lillian.

When she was thirteen, Lillian was sent to stay with the Harp family in their Woollahra home as part of a scheme set up by the AWB. Mrs Harp had been a good friend of Mr Jeffrey, one of the AWB supervisors based at La Perouse, and she had written a letter to Mr Jeffrey offering a 'holiday' to an Aboriginal girl from the outback. The supposed 'holiday', which incidentally was deemed a great success by the AWB, was later described in a full-page article and letter, purported to be written by Lillian, in *Dawn Magazine*.[87] In spite of her affections for the Harp family, Lillian always maintained, right up until the time she passed away in 2005, that she never wrote such a letter.[88] The following is the letter in question.

> It was one afternoon when I came home from school and my sister Marjorie said, 'You are going to Sydney.' I was so excited I started to tell everyone, but they wouldn't believe me. A few days later Mr Green came

around with Mrs Grant and made all the arrangements with my mother. Eventually the day came and I set out by train. We travelled all night and all the places we passed through looked very nice from the window of the train. When morning came, we were still travelling, and Mrs Grant and I thought that the train was running late. At last, we arrived at Central and Mr and Mrs Jeffrey were waiting to meet us and take us out to La Perouse where we had breakfast. Later Mr Jeffrey took me over to Mrs Harp's place where I met Miranda, Aviva and Joe. That day we went to Bondi Junction. We went to different places every day and in the next two weeks we went to Koala Park and the Zoo. We played tennis in Cooper Park and went rowing on the Lane Cove River. But I think the most exciting outing was the Jazz concert. Mrs Harp took Miranda and I around to the stage door and we got the actors' autographs. I love Sydney and all the children I met. Miss Bell took Miranda and I to Manly and other friends took us into the City. I had never seen such lovely shops. I do want to thank the Welfare Board for letting me come down and for paying my fare, and I also want to thank Mrs Harp for having me to stay with her. I have never had such a lovely holiday before.[89]

Lillian told her family that she was not expected to work for Mrs Harp on that 'holiday' and she was made to feel like a guest of the family. However, when she returned to Sydney a few years later, Lillian did end up working as a domestic for the Harp family, before finding a job at the Sweetacres confectionary factory in Rosebery, and later at the Peters ice cream factory in Redfern. Within a year of Lillian's 'holiday', Marj began working for the Harps and, like Lillian, Marj did not experience any malice or distrust for the Harps; rather, she felt sorry for them, especially for Mrs Harp, who told horrible stories about the concentration camps during World War II, and who taught her how to cook Jewish meals. And so, the policies of assimilation were set into action.

CHAPTER 7

'A Choice of Three'

Triangle, trio & three
So, what do they truly mean?
It derives from organisations
Of a plan A, B and C

For instance, a word like passion
It's in everything that we do
With this graphic line connection
Let me try and show it to you

Triangle wedge of decision
From one point to another
In a box of word connections
From each corner to the other

Everyone I know applies it
In life, in work, in play
It's a driving force to contend with
And we use it everyday

Not just in tender moments
But in anger when filled with rage
In silent sentimental sadness
In not being bold and brave

And not just the flip side of opposite
Like the other side of a coin
But an extra point to go to
When deciding which line to join

A half-way mark to consider
What option is the best?
To resolve a situation
If it's causing emotional unrest

A three-way intersection
Like a sudden fork in the road
Left, right and centre
Sit down, stand up or go

And let's not forget the hours
'Tween sunset and sunrise
I believe it's known as twilight
A dream-like state of mind

In the middle of a court room
A-game, or field of play
Close third-party involvement
Ends-up having the final say

Majority over minority
Rules justice should prevail
In every set of circumstance
1-2-3 will tilt the scale

So, our world has so much to offer
With odds and ends combined
This middle ground method of mystery
Is a deadly line of design.

Jimmy's proposal to Marj was rather clumsy, but it was successful just the same. He had bought the ring, taken it to her place and got down on one knee to propose but, because he fumbled with the ring, Marj had to help him along. She took it from his hand, put it on her own finger, and never took it off from that day onwards. On the day Marj took Jimmy to her home in Walgett to meet her family, it was fortunate that everyone was there – both her parents, her grandmother, and her seven sisters and two brothers (Cecil, Elaine, Lillian, Marie, Douglas, Lorraine, Doreen, Valerie and Jennifer). Jimmy and Marj had been dating for about three years before he finally popped the question. He had already noticed how close her family was and thought himself lucky to be welcomed by them – not just by the immediate family members but also by Marj's extended family, who travelled for miles to meet Marj's 'intended'. Marj's family seemed so different to his own family, who by now were mainly alienated from each other following the death of their mother Sissy.

The train ride from Sydney to Walgett took about twenty-three hours, which was something of a novelty for Jimmy, who was only used to train trips of a few hours to get to the South

Coast and back. The long, straight, flat journey across the dry arid regions of the north-west plains was in stark contrast to the winding mountainous and seaside train trips he was accustomed to. When they finally arrived in Walgett, members of the Peters family greeted them at the railway station and then they jam-packed the taxi with people and luggage. The family group that met them included Marj's mother, sister Lillian and her brother Douglas, and baby Valerie, whom Jimmy nursed on his lap on the taxi ride home.

A few days later, Jimmy and Marj were married at St Peters Church of England, on Marj's twenty-first birthday, 19 August 1957 – the groom a tall, slim man (Jimmy always referred to himself as 'lanky') with tight, curly hair, and the bride much shorter, with thick, wavy black hair.

Jimmy's best man was Claude (Candy) Williams, a singer and close friend of Jimmy and Marj's back in Sydney, and his other groomsman was Marj's younger brother Cecil. Marj's father, Henry, walked her down the aisle and her bridesmaids were cousin Maureen Simpson and sister Elaine Peters. It would have been a quiet ceremony if it were not for Marj's teary-eyed, circus-performing uncle Bilidju (aka Abdul the Fire-Eater), who cried loudly all through the ceremony, calling out his niece's nickname, 'Midge'.

Yes, it's one day in one's life that one could never forget. It was just wonderful. It was a simple gathering at a quiet country church, just two streets away from her mum and dad's house, filled to the brim with Marj's relatives. The reception was held at the house. The photos were taken at the photographer's house, which was, again, in the neighbourhood. It was a big event, because all the family on my

Jimmy with his father Kunkus Little and Dora Williams. Nowra, 1955.

ABOVE: *The movie poster for* Shadow of the Boomerang *(1960), Jimmy's first acting role. This poster, which has been annotated by Jimmy, came from the scrapbook he kept.*

BELOW: *More clippings from Jimmy's scrapbook.*

ABOVE: *Jimmy being inducted into the ARIA Hall of Fame with Marcia Hines and Andrew Farriss (of INXS), 1999.* [Jim Trifyllis/Newspix/News Ltd.]

LEFT: *Jimmy and Kylie Minogue. The pair recorded 'Bury Me Deep in Love' together in 2001 for a Festival Mushroom Records album titled* Corroboration. [David Anderson]

RIGHT: *Jimmy performing on stage with his brother Fred and sisters Monica and Betty. St Marys.*

Jimmy with his grandson James Henry Little, 2004.
[Jeff Darmanin/Newspix/News Ltd.]

LEFT: *Jimmy with manager Buzz Bidstrup, 2008.*

BELOW: *Jimmy and Buzz inspect the construction of the Purple Bus, a self-contained dialysis unit on wheels, which the Jimmy Little Foundation provided initial funding for.*

Jimmy with his daughter Frances Peters-Little, 2010.
[Juno Gemes ©/Juno Gemes Archive]

Left: *Jimmy and Marj Little's wedding, 1957. From left to right: Claude Williams, Elaine Peters, Jimmy Little, Marj Little, Henry Peters, Maureen Simpson, Cecil Peters and Doreen Peters.*

Right: *Jimmy with Marj, James Henry and Frances, celebrating Jimmy and Marj's 50th wedding anniversary, 2007.*

Left: *Jimmy and Marj celebrating their 50th wedding anniversary, 2007.*

Jimmy's memorial concert at the Sydney Opera House, 2012. Jimmy's grandson James Henry sings, supported by the Jimmy Little Trio (Tony Green, Doug Peters and Cyril Green). Seated: Deborah Cheetham, Esther Cohen and Frances Peters-Little. [Peter Rae/The Sydney Morning Herald]

The Walgett Water Tower, completed in 2020. The mural of Jimmy was painted by artists Jenny McCracken & Frank Wright and was based on a photograph taken by John Elliott. [Zest Events International]

wife's side were there in great numbers, with great enthusiasm, and it was really special. I mean, you think of a wedding as being special anyway, like a twenty-first birthday party, but when it happens to you and you're the centre of the attraction of the whole event, then it becomes doubly enjoyable and memorable. Our wedding was the beginning of a wonderful relationship after a three-year courtship. I think Marj and I were kind of in awe about the whole thing. That's how we felt, and it had been a grand time becoming Mr and Mrs Little.

When Jimmy and Marj returned to Sydney, they found a bedsit apartment on Moore Park Road in Paddington. When Marj became pregnant, Jimmy knew he would have to find a job that paid better than the timber yards and that they also had to find a bigger flat now that a baby was on the way. While Marj was in the Paddington Royal Hospital for Women, Jimmy found a bedsit in Lawson Street, Redfern, close to the Redfern railway station.

Paddington was one of the main hospitals for maternity in the eastern suburbs area. I was day-working in a timber yard, and my brother Freddy and I went to visit my wife in hospital a couple of days after she was admitted, and I walked into the usual waiting room and one nurse came out and said something to the effect of, 'Good evening, Mr Little, your wife and daughter are doing fine,' and I nearly fell over. I was blown away with the thought. I was going to see my wife, who [as far as I knew] was still expecting. Our daughter Frances was six weeks' premature, and that was a surprise. I just couldn't get in there quick enough to hold her and look at her. She had thick, long black hair, straight, straight, long jet-black hair, and it matched her skin, her olive skin, and she looked just absolutely beautiful. So that was a grand moment.

Jimmy was all of twenty years old when Frances Claire was born. She was named after both Jimmy's mother, Frances, and Marj's mother, whose middle name was Claire. When Frances Claire was born, Jimmy wrote a song for his two-week-old baby daughter. With Jimmy and Pat expected to write and record their own compositions for the B Side of any record, Jimmy wrote a song in response to the birth of his daughter – 'Frances Claire' – one of the sixteen songs he recorded.

She's our own little girl
All we have in this world
She brightens our heart everyday
You should see when she smiles
Though she knows all the while
That no-one could steal her away
She's all we desire
And no money could ever buy her
Like a doll with her silk flowing hair
On her shawl lying there
We decided calling her
Our beautiful
Frances Claire

The thought that Jimmy might have to give up his music never even entered Marj's mind and she did nothing to discourage Jimmy from focusing more on his singing career. Even when he needed

Jimmy with daughter Frances in Birchgrove, Sydney, 1962.

to go away for a while, Marj's grandmother Clara would take the twenty-three-hour train trip down from Walgett to Redfern so that she could keep a watch over her first great-granddaughter.

Between recording and performing in clubs and hotels and appearing on radio, Jimmy found that Ted Quigg was increasingly showing a serious interest in him, lining Jimmy up for more singing jobs, and then becoming his manager. Quigg became a key figure in the lives of Jimmy and Marj, but Marj never lost her scepticism of people in the music industry. In Marj's mind, having a manager like Ted Quigg had its benefits as well as its drawbacks. She understood Quigg already had connections in the Sydney music scene with artists such as Col Joye, Frank Ifield, Judy Stone, Lonnie Lee and many others via his *On The Trail* show on radio 2SM, and while she knew this would be good for Jimmy's career, she and Jimmy firmly valued and guarded their independence. This was Australia in the 1960s, when many people were unaccustomed to seeing a forthright Aboriginal woman in charge, but Jimmy saw his wife as a business partner as well as a life partner, the perfect combination. There were many, however, who did not know how to tolerate her forthright approach.

Marj was firm and strong and much more business minded than me. I was more the artistic, free-flowing creative kind of person who looked at life as being there to enjoy, if one managed the things at my disposal and put them into place. That was the artist at work, whereas in business it's another form of artist at work. So we were like two bookends looking after all the loose ends and making sure the middle was filled in and properly run. In fact, I think we were a formidable team, who were put together as part of destiny, but we still had to work at it. We still had to be the lovebirds that we wanted to be all the way through. We wanted to be kind and gentle and soft-hearted and reasonable and fair, and we had to be sometimes a little tough with people that we dealt with, but it was all for the better.

I suppose people were critical of Marj, but no-one ever said anything to me personally about my wife's attitude in the business. I know how she spoke on the phone to people and how she spoke in person to people, very businesslike. Some people who wanted me were more determined in their own way to get me to do what they wanted, and when they didn't get their own way with Marj at the helm, then they would back off and realise that they were dealing with fair-minded, strong-minded people.

Having grown up knowing there were so many other Aboriginal talents out there of his age, Jimmy suggested to Quigg that he (Quigg) might like to meet them. One was Jimmy's brother Freddy, who had a velvety, sweet voice like Jimmy's and who had now arrived in Sydney. Quigg liked what he heard and saw an opportunity to capitalise on the two brothers performing together on the Sydney circuit. Although the brothers performed together occasionally, they both had different interests and chose to go solo in the long term.

Since Quigg lived in Sydney's western suburbs and ran his musical agency from his home in Granville, he persuaded the two brothers to live and work closer to where he lived, so he could keep a close eye on them. In keeping with Quigg's wishes, Freddy found work at the Lidcombe railway yards, and Jimmy found work on Parramatta Road in Auburn. So, Jimmy, Marj and baby Frances moved to Granville for a brief time, leaving behind the inner-city suburbs of Sydney.

It was during this period that, to Jimmy and Marj's delight, Quigg was able to line Jimmy up with his acting spot in *Shadow of the Boomerang*. It hadn't been a difficult decision for Jimmy to leave his day job behind to be on set with the cast and crew on the cattle station near Moree, as this meant that Marj and daughter Frances could stay with Marj's family in Walgett, which was a two-and-a-half-hour drive from Moree. Spending time with Marj's family, it was easy for Jimmy to see where Marj inherited her strong attitude. Like Jimmy, she came from a family of resolute Aboriginal people who had endured many hardships. Also, like Jimmy's parents, Marj's parents had always followed work and lived wherever they could. The story of how they got to where they were was just as difficult as Jimmy's, but in a very different way.

Marj was born in 1936 to Henry and Doreen Peters, three years before the outbreak of World War II. Marj's parents were barely twenty years old when they married at Angledool police station in 1933. The reason they were married in a police station, according to Doreen, was that they were not allowed to marry in a church because they were Aboriginal.[90] As if the insult of being rejected by the church was not enough, the wedding ceremony itself was sullied further by the police, who slung insults, threatening Henry and intimidating him because he insisted on using his father's surname, which was Peters. The police argued that Henry was not a real Peters and should only be allowed to use his mother's maiden name, which was Foster. Henry stood his ground, proved the police wrong and was allowed to use his rightful name of Peters.

Marj was Henry and Doreen's second child, and she shared their same level of stubbornness. Even the circumstances of her birth may have prepared her for what lay ahead. While Marj was still in her mother's womb, the Angledool mission's manager, Donaldson,[91] ordered all the Aboriginal people on the mission to climb aboard cattle trucks in the middle of the night. It was the dead of winter in July 1936. While one cattle truck transported half of the people to Brewarrina Mission (aka Dodge City), the other truck transported the rest to Gingie Mission, 13 kilometres outside Walgett (although Henry and Doreen later moved to Lightning Ridge). But it was Gingie Mission where Marj was born, in a tent, one early wintery morning a month after Donaldson shifted them off Angledool.

Marj's father, Henry, came from Bangate Station, born to parents Benjamin and Dahlia Peters in May 1914. Benjamin Peters was a 'full-blooded' traditional Yuwaalaraay clever fella who got his surname from his father, Hippai Peters, also known as Peter Hippai, who played a pivotal role in the storytelling of Yuwaalaraay cultural practices in Katie Langloh Parker's *My Bush Book*. Henry's mother was Dahlia Foster, who had fairer skin, and got her surname, it is said, from being connected to the Foster family – one of the first early White settlers in the area. Dahlia Foster is also recognised as one of the descendants of the bushranger Captain Thunderbolt.

On the other side of the family, Marj's mother, Doreen Claire, was born near Walgett,[92] on the Namoi Reserve[93] in 1913. Marj's grandmother, Clara Frail, originally came from Cobar and married Jack 'Smart Guy' Simpson in Brewarrina in 1911. Jack was born in 1888 on Boorooma Station, 70 kilometres west of Walgett. Jack Simpson's father was most likely the White station manager of Boorooma, John Simpson. His mother, as far as we know, was 'part

Aboriginal' and part descendant of an Afghani cameleer who camped at Brewarrina Station on his way to the Bourke Camel Station.

Smart Guy and Clara Simpson had five children: two daughters – Doreen, born in 1913, and Lulu, born in 1912 – and three sons – Jack, born in 1911, George, in 1914, and Archibald (aka Bilidju), in 1915. Like Jimmy's family, they were all entertainers in their own right. Doreen and Lulu were singers, while their brother George was a dancer who also sang and played the spoons and 'clicked his fingers' – creating a percussive sound by clicking or snapping the fingers is common in many cultures and was popular in Vaudeville at that time. Their other two brothers, Jack and Bilidju were magicians. Jack performed several card tricks and did a bit of boxing from time to time in the circus shows, and Bilidju, joined the Sole Brothers Circus, performing all over Australia as 'Abdul the Fire-Eater'.

Marj's grandmother Clara, who was also known as Topsy, was born in 1890 to Tilly Riley, whose mother, Emily, was a 'full-blooded' Aboriginal woman from Carowra Tank, and whose White father, name unknown, was from Nymagee. Issues relating to caste or skin colour mattered deeply in that era for a number of reasons, the first being that a child who was not a 'full-blood' Aboriginal person was more likely to be illegitimate and raised by a single mother. Just as Clara was fair skinned, so too was Marj's mother, Doreen. It was Doreen's fair complexion which later made her a source of research for an American eugenicist by the name of Charles Davenport, in 1914.[94] He was responsible for performing a series of eye-colouring and skin-colouring tests on Doreen, who was one year old at the time.

Clara was raised by Tilly and her stepfather, George Frail, whose family name she took. Frail was a bullocky driver on Meadows Station at the time when eighteen-year-old Clara was captured by a White man by the name of Frank Akers and taken 40 kilometres away from her family. Being eighteen years old in those days meant she was underage. Tilly and George reported their daughter Clara missing, and within three days she was found by the police on the property with Akers. Akers was arrested for rape and kidnap and, in a Cobar court of petty sessions packed to the rim and with an all-White male jury, he was acquitted of the charge. The judge then deemed it best for Clara to be taken a further 300 kilometres away to Brewarrina Aboriginal Station, away from her parents, to serve out her duties as a domestic servant. Shortly after her arrival, in 1908, Clara gave birth to a daughter, Fredia Frail, who has never been found since.

Marj's mother Doreen always carried the hurt and injustices her own mother Clara went through and she passed those stories down to her children. Doreen also talked about the years she lost when she was thirteen and was apprenticed to work for property owners: she had to wake up early every morning to make sure the cows were milked before the family had their breakfast and was only allowed to go to bed after she had scrubbed their floors and cleared their dishes from the table at night; during this time she was never allowed to eat with others, nor was she able to see any of her family members for several years. With this family history, it was understandable that Marj learned to be mistrustful of others, to never back down from a fight and to take a stand against unfairness. It was those strengths that Jimmy loved most about his partner, and he was deeply protective of Marj when she became physically unwell in the years to come.

A lot of people might wonder why it was that I never shied away from Marj. When she's upset about something and is worried about something, then I will calm her down with my quiet care and explain the best thing that will happen, and the worst thing that will happen – and we're going to work through it. Then she'll relax and realise that the mountain is not as big as it seems. Then the reverse of that is if I get a little disheartened about something and I think I've lost my chance, my opportunity, and I get kind of a little cranky with myself, then she will give me the strength, with her fire and passion, to say, 'Listen, that miss is a blessing in disguise'. So we know each other pretty well, and we were able to support each other again from both ends of our viewing of the situation.

CHAPTER 8

'Royal Telephone'

Telephone to glory, oh, what joy divine!
I can feel the current moving on the line,
Made by God the Father for His very own,
You may talk to Jesus on this royal telephone.

Central's never 'busy', always on the line.
You may hear from heaven almost any time.
'Tis a royal service, free for one and all.
When you get in trouble, give this royal line a call.

Telephone to glory, oh, what joy divine!
I can feel the current moving on the line,
Made by God the Father for His very own,
You may talk to Jesus on this royal telephone.

There will be no charges, telephone is free,
It was built for service, just for you and me.
There will be no waiting on this royal line,
Telephone to glory always answers just in time.

> *Telephone to glory, oh, what joy divine!*
> *I can feel the current moving on the line,*
> *Made by God the Father for His very own,*
> *You may talk to Jesus on this royal telephone.*

By the time Jimmy recorded his hit song 'Royal Telephone' with Festival Records in 1963, he was already well on his way to stardom. Once Jimmy had commenced recording with Festival Records he never strayed far from the label, even though in 1959 he was offered the chance of moving overseas and recording in the United States. The offer was tempting, but Jimmy and Marj declined, telling Oscar Davis, a well-known American entrepreneur and manager to Hank Williams, that Jimmy was more interested in seeing where this new and exciting Australian music industry was heading. Jimmy's rejection of the big offer to go overseas to promote his career was noted by a journalist for *Dawn Magazine* in 1959, who wrote:

> A former Nowra bean-picker who earned 30s a week only four years ago is being hailed as a star by a visiting American promoter, the man who 'discovered' Elvis Presley. The former Nowra boy is part-aboriginal [sic] Jimmy Little, 21, now living in Lackey-street, Granville, Sydney. He shared top billing with American stars in a Western show called 'Grand Ole Opry', at the Sydney Stadium on March 5, 6 and 7. The American promoter who thinks Jimmy Little has a great future in show business is Oscar Davis, a well-known theatrical entrepreneur in the US. He found Elvis Presley singing in a small cabaret in Memphis, Tennessee in 1956, made

him a star and was his exploitation manager for three years. Mr Davis arrived in Sydney recently on the lookout for talent to support the US stars who appeared in 'Grand Ole Opry' including Roy Acuff, known as 'King of Country Music', in the US where he has sold more than 40 million records; the Wilburn Brothers, top Western recording artists; and lovely blonde June Webb, whose discs have figured on both the popular and Western hit parades in the US. Mr Davis said: 'I spotted Jimmy on TV just after I arrived in Sydney. I found out that he was singing in a hall at Auburn the next night, so I went out to see him. I signed him up immediately for 'Grand Ole Opry'. He explained, 'Grand Ole Opry' is a Western show which has been staged in America for 33 years. It is also broadcast over 400 stations every Saturday night. The show has been the birthplace of such stars as Dinah Shore, Pat Hone, Jerry Lee Lewis, the Everly Brothers, as well as Elvis Presley. I have already booked Jimmy to tour New Zealand. I think he has a great voice and real 'star quality'. Jimmy has a lot in common with Elvis. His singing style is different but he has the same dedicated attitude towards his career. Elvis never got too big for his shoes and I know Jimmy is the same.[95]

Although he did perform for the Australian and New Zealand leg of the *Grand Ole Opry* show, Jimmy's instincts not to travel to the United States and to stick with an emerging Australian rock and roll industry may have paid off. Jimmy never regretted his decision not to move overseas, saying he thought he would be a little fish in a big pond there. Throughout his career he often referred to himself as a 'proud home-grown product', and he kept a level head about how far his 'success' might take him, saying that 'he did not need to be at the top of the tree, because the fruit that hung from the lower branches would taste just as sweet'.

Oscar Davis returned to the United States with New Zealand–born hillbilly singer Tex Morton in place of Jimmy. Morton did end up performing and recording at the *Grand Ole Opry* in Tennessee, touring his show on the road in the United States, with Oscar Davis as his manager, but Morton returned to Australia after Oscar Davis had a heart attack and was left paralysed from a stroke.

The other reason Jimmy did not want to go to the United States under Oscar Davis's managerial control was that he was concerned he may have had to confine his musical style to that of a country-style singer. He had always yearned for the musical flexibility of being able to move between the various genres of music and felt the time was ripe for him and many other people in the Australian music industry to flourish.

The nation became more free-flowing and then the mums and dads of the time, who were very reserved and very restricted and very concerned about the nation, were coming to be open to all sorts of unwise opportunities. It was really a coming of age.

This was a period that saw great change in Australian society due to the evolution of popular culture and Aboriginal rights. Specifically, this aspect of entertainment introduced major cultural changes. New ideas were adopted towards entertainment in Australia and ultimately this helped to shape modern Australian society,[96] and

Jimmy became interested in what he saw as a teenage revolution. To Jimmy, the world previously only consisted of adults and children, but now there were teenagers, and they were the ones who mostly flocked to his shows and followed the Australian music scene.

That was the first teenage music in the world. Before that, it was just children's music and adult music; there was no in between, no teen music. So here I was, I was twenty-two, and all the other performers of my generation were all just out of high school, and we were just becoming young adults, pioneering our path, that had never been pioneered before, and the rush and hysteria of the public who accepted it wholeheartedly frightened the adults. The parents and the grandparents thought, 'Our young people are going crazy'. We were the centre of attraction of that, and it was exciting, and also a little bit disturbing and a little bit frightening. Then it settled down, the big wave settled down and everybody just accepted the big wave was going to be there, flooding the land emotionally with happy music.

In the Festival days, the songs that I sang for the public were current, popular, and also popular evergreens, songs of yesteryear. Because I sang these songs in my live performances, the record company said, 'Sing what you sing to the people and put that on record,' and so we did. That meant singing golden oldies, songs down memory lane, and they were a mix of popular, classics and country music songs, and folk songs, story songs and bush ballads about the nature of our country, rural Australia. So a nice variety and mix of songs were recorded during my contract years with Festival Records. I would pick the songs, but Festival Records was responsible for the arranging and distribution. All I had to do was learn the songs, arrive and record them, and the rest was done by them.

Four years after he signed with Festival Records, it was suggested that Jimmy might like to listen to a hymn recorded and made popular by the well-known American actor/singer Burl Ives. Ives was known for his acting roles in films like *So Dear to My Heart* (1949), *Cat on a Hot Tin Roof* (1958) and *The Big Country* (1958), for which he won an Academy Award for Best Supporting Actor. Ives, an itinerant singer and banjoist already well-known to American audiences, launched his own radio show, *The Wayfaring Stranger*, popularising traditional folk songs, before he successfully crossed over into country music, recording hits such as 'A Little Bitty Tear' and 'Funny Way of Laughin'. Despite his popularity and success, though, he came under scrutiny by the House Committee on Un-American Activities and was blacklisted as an entertainer, for supposedly having Communist ties with folk singer Peter Seeger.

Frederick M. Lehman wrote 'Royal Telephone' in 1919 as a hymn. Lehman was born in Germany in 1868, emigrated to America with his family at the age of four, and at the age of eleven 'came to Christ' after a 'heavenly' experience while walking through a crabapple grove.[97] The lyrics that he wrote for 'Royal Telephone' were embedded in the strong beliefs of southern Pentecostals, who thought of a 'royal telephone' as a way of communicating with God.[98] Whether or not the song had its roots in southern Pentecostal hymns did not seem to bother Australian youths or the Australian music industry too much. In the early to mid 1960s, approximately 88 per cent of the Australian population was deemed to be Christian.[99]

Album artwork for *Royal Telephone* EP, 1965.

With Burl Ives already having made 'Royal Telephone' a hit in America in 1962, and with the song also receiving airplay on Australian radio in Western Australia, this led Festival Records producer Joe Halford to make the suggestion that Jimmy might like to record the song and make it his own. At that time Festival Records commissioned well-known Hungarian-born Australian pianist, conductor, composer and arranger Tommy Tycho. When Tycho was fifteen (in 1943), he and his parents were interned in a German forced labour camp and he was lucky to survive. The Australian artists with whom he worked include Peter Allen, Ricky May, Olivia Newton-John, Julie Anthony, John Farnham, Anthony Warlow, Jill Perryman, Barry Crocker, Kamahl and many more. He also worked with overseas performers such as Sammy Davis Jr, Nat King Cole, Shirley Bassey, Louis Armstrong, Jerry Lewis, Frank Sinatra and many others.

Tycho was at the top of his game in 1963. He was the musical director at the Seven Network and had already been involved in several Royal Command Performances and conducted the ABC symphony orchestras. Festival Records and Tycho agreed to arrange a new version for Jimmy that would be more commercial and less hymnal. As Tycho explains:

> The recording company said here's this very young talented Aboriginal boy, with a great voice and you've got to find a good popular song for him, and so we produced this Lutheran hymn called 'Royal Telephone', which talks about us getting in touch with God, and then he began to modernise and upgrade the lyrics, and it was my task to write the tune, and eventually orchestrate and record it for Jimmy. It's his signature tune, and the rest is history.[100]

The song rocketed up the charts for Jimmy, who thought of it as an upbeat gospel tune rather than a hymn. He had not anticipated the outcomes it would have for him, and the impact it would have on his reputation among Australian audiences, who were mostly Christian at the time. Jimmy's version of 'Royal Telephone' sold over seventy-five thousand copies, and by November 1964 it peaked on the charts at number one in Sydney and number three in Melbourne, outplaying Burl Ives's version in Australia. In 1964 *Everybody's Magazine* declared Jimmy Little as Australia's Pop Artist of the Year, while the Beatles, who were touring Australia in 1964, were awarded the Most Popular Overseas Artists.[101] Another popular magazine, *Australian Women's Weekly*, had a music writer by the name of Bob Rogers, who described Jimmy's version as 'a sincere ballad with a religious feeling', and in only three weeks the record was rising to the top all over Australia, as one of the fastest-selling records of the year. Not only was 'Royal Telephone' awarded three gold certifications (that is, three gold records) by Festival Records, Jimmy's version of the song was also voted the Best Male Vocal Disk in the Tunetable Awards for Australia's first disk awards from a major radio source for home-produced disks.[102]

'Royal Telephone' was a popular request by the public listening in the city of Perth. People would ring the station and request this song called 'Royal Telephone'. It wasn't my version. It was an album version by a singer called Burl Ives. Burl Ives is well known to the world musically. Whenever a song is popular, by an overseas artist, local record companies would get their local artists to do what they call a cover version. We would do an Aussie version of it. So the record company got me to do a cover version of the Burl Ives popular [song] 'Royal Telephone', and it really took off, like a rocket to the moon. People loved it. It was just a great time to do what we call a cover version of a song that captured the imagination of the public, and won me three gold records.

Festival Records' producers may well have come up with the idea of Jimmy recording 'Royal Telephone' to capitalise on the success Jimmy had had in the feature film *Shadow of the Boomerang* three years earlier. The film was produced by American evangelist and ordained Southern Baptist minister Billy Graham's film arm, World Wide Pictures. Throughout the production of the *Shadow of the Boomerang* and its subsequent success, though, Jimmy never actually met Billy Graham.

A year before Jimmy recorded 'Royal Telephone', Festival Records produced an EP called *The Way of The Cross*. The cover featured an image of Jimmy looking like he was wearing a clerical collar, standing in front of a mock stained-glass window with a sacrificial cross. Jimmy recorded many other Festival Records albums to follow 'Royal Telephone', such as *Sing to Glory* (1963) and *Onward Christian Soldier* (1965), so it was highly understandable that people took Jimmy to be a rampant Christian. Not everyone agreed to play 'Royal Telephone' back in the 1960s; in fact radio station 2SM put a ban on it. Between 1937 and the 1990s, 2SM was owned by the Catholic Broadcasting Company and as 'Royal Telephone' was a southern American Pentecostal hymn, they wouldn't play it. For Jimmy, singing a gospel tune was more a case of going along with Festival Records' marketing strategy, and he thought there was nothing unusual about singing gospel songs. They were already popular with singers like Elvis Presley, Jerry Lee Lewis, Mahalia Jackson, and many others who were already doing it in the United States. Perhaps the most common negative response came from those who saw the song as being a blatant 'selling of Christianity' to the masses, particularly Aboriginal people. Aboriginal people had many reasons to criticise what Christianity had done to them through the assimilation policies and the policing of Aboriginal lives on missions and Christian institutions.

I think some people may have thought I was pushing religion and frowned upon me singing a religious song, but I thought, in music, that 'Royal Telephone' was much like 'Amazing Grace', 'Just a Closer Walk with Thee' and all those fine songs of faith that are out there for people to sing with and listen to. I wasn't influenced by any particular affiliation, because I just grew up in the faith of my own Aboriginality teachings, from our tribal ways, which I combined with the Christian teachings.

However, this view of Jimmy as an assimilated Aboriginal man whitewashed by Christianity and assimilation in general, is apparent in a film by Aboriginal filmmaker Tracey Moffatt three decades later. Moffatt has Jimmy performing 'Royal Telephone' in her film *Night Cries*, with the purpose of having 'Royal Telephone' function as a 'grating' effect within the film. Jimmy and Marj did not anticipate that this was the intention of the filmmaker, whom they thought was just being respectful of Jimmy and his song. As Moffatt describes it:

> I wanted to end the film ... leaving the daughter [played by Marcia Langton] in an emotional state, and then bring in Jimmy Little with his boppy song so that it would grate even more. He offers this Christian healing, which can be so unwelcome and inappropriate at times. At the same time, I don't want to make fun of Jimmy or his Christianity. I present him as he is in real life ... but, in fact, he's not really soothing at all, but grating.[103]

From Jimmy's point of view, he never thought of himself as offering Christian healing to anyone, but sang the song because it was marketable at the time and he liked it. He had no reason to dislike Christian songs or gospel music and grew up watching his mother and his siblings singing hymns on Sundays and considered it a good thing. On the other hand, his father Kunkus may have been less convinced of the healing powers of church music, but he did not mind his children getting a Christian education.

I don't remember early day preaching in and around Woorigee when I was there. But back at Cummeragunja we would go to Sunday school fairly often, because of the missionary school. But then I always had a sense of religion in my mind and my heart, in my dealing with nature on a daily basis. I remember things like animals and insects and flowers and trees and birds and sky and rain, and all these things were nature's gift. To me, they in themselves were a spiritual comforting from the creator. So I always felt that in my surroundings I was living in a spiritual stream of respecting life for what it was. I didn't have to read the Bible or hear about it in hymns to be conscious about the fact that I was living a spiritual life. It all felt natural just to be appreciative of all that creativity around me. But certainly, when we did sing gospel songs on those few occasions that I witnessed and participated in, I was certainly deeply involved in trying to understand a deeper level of Christianity.

The tide of success and fame was thrust upon an eager and perhaps naive Jimmy, but at no time did he shy away from the responsibility. He had not taken himself too seriously as a star, but, throughout his career, he always managed to maintain a generosity, kindness and humility for which he will forever be remembered. His Australian pop star friends (like Australian pop and country music singer Judy Stone[104]) described Jimmy as someone who had a still presence when he went out on stage, and who single-handedly quietened the audiences after she and others had the crowds dancing in their seats. Jimmy's other contemporary, Australian rockabilly pioneer Lonnie Lee,[105] said that Jimmy's performances, whether he was doing country, pop or gospel, always had a truthfulness about them. And when people like pioneer rock singer-songwriter and musician Col Joye[106] and his band, the Joy Boys, toured with Jimmy, they were the ones who would confront the club managers if, on learning that Jimmy was Aboriginal, the managers refused to have Jimmy enter their premises – they would perform at jails, nursing homes and institutions that detained Aboriginal children, such as the Cootamundra Domestic Training Home for Aboriginal Girls.[107]

> The Aboriginal girls' home in Cootamundra – Col and I went up there to entertain. We went to hospitals together, the town halls and shows. We felt the same about our craft as being, belonging to the people. So we were kind of like brothers, in terms of having the same heartbeat for our industry and the people we entertained.[108]

Col Joye was also instrumental in talent-spotting Aboriginal singer Vic Simms, whom he saw at a 'football social' in Sydney. Simms went on to have his own fame, recording his first single at the age of fifteen, and his first album, *The Loner*, in 1973. Reflecting on his own success, Jimmy said:

> I never dreamed of becoming an idol in a musical sense. In many places I went to, I was mobbed. It was frightening, and it was fun. People wanted souvenirs from you, they wanted autographs, and they wanted to write to you and become penfriends and all of

that. I'd even go to people's homes, and they'd have pictures of me plastered all over their walls. There were fan clubs and all that. And the mailman would deliver bags of mail to my home, and me and my wife and daughter would read all the letters together. It was an exciting time to be in that world of music ... A tidal wave was washing over, a hysterical Australia en masse.

The time was ripe for the new musical revolution that was taking place in Australia, with its own musical talents, its own recording company, and television variety shows like *Bandstand, Six O'Clock Rock, Words and Music, Youth Show, Keith Walshe, The John Konrads Show, The Lorrae Desmond Show, Tea for Two, The Johnny O'Keefe Show/Sing, Sing, Sing, The Bryan Davies Show, Teen Scene, The Go!! Show,* Johnny Young's *Young Talent Time, Kommotion, Club Seventeen, It's All Happening, It's A Gas, Uptight, Where the Action Is, GTK* and *Hitscene.*

Col Joye and Johnny O'Keefe were the premier rock and roll icons of the time. They ended up with their own television shows and their own road shows, and the rest of us were guests on their shows, both live and on television. I did most of my road touring with Col Joye and the Joy Boys, and in those tours there were people like Judy Stone, the Allen Brothers, Dig Richards, Judy Cannon, Colin Cooper and Jay Justin, and then I'd remember seeing Warren Williams, Lonnie Lee, Kevin Todd, Laurel Lee and Patsy Ann Noble on tour and on television. I can see all their faces now – the Delltones, the Crescents, the Fawns, the Graduates, and of course Johnny O'Keefe and the Deejays.

And then on top of all of that, you had all the other cities with their performers. Brisbane acts as well, and all the Melbourne acts and all the Adelaide acts. Every city had all their own teenage stars, and they kept on coming. We were not making a fortune, but we were making a lot of friends and a lot of fans. Later on, as we became more professional in our performances, we then entered the nightclub scene, the clubs of our suburbia. Those clubs in Sydney and New South Wales particularly – we had poker machines, the one-armed bandits that gave the club a budget for live entertainment every weekend. It was a heady time for the busy popular artists that there were and, as we all got a little older and a little more settled into this big new industry, a lot of the performers became star performers and had their own band and their own shows, including me. So, I became a star performer out of those days and had my own show and my own band and I've still got that today. So, it's been a long, hard road.

There may have been many opportunities for Jimmy to get caught up in a rowdier lifestyle, but it was not in his gentle nature. This was not because he was a devout Christian or anything like that; it was more because he led a quiet life and had other obligations that kept him in check.

Unlike a lot of the other people my age, I was in my early twenties, I was a married man, and I was a father, so there were stabilising points of my life that meant I didn't get swept away with it all. I went with the flow, but I was able to step back from the rush of it all and realise that it's all going to be around for a long time, and I'll enjoy it in little doses rather than big doses, and I didn't go down the waterfall with the rush of it all. I kept going across the stream, from bank to bank, in an emotional sense, and enjoying it as a young married man. The public, as I analysed it later, they didn't feel that while I wasn't available – I wasn't this bachelor on the loose – I was this other form of attraction. I was like a big brother, a successful member of the family.

And I didn't want this time to be just a flash in the pan, over and done with. I said, 'This is what I've been thinking of as a boy at school'. I wanted to be a success as a singer, and I was proving that point to myself and to my immediate family that I have qualified to become a recognisable and popular singer and I wanted to make an honest living out of that, and I didn't want to use it or abuse it or let it become manipulative to my nature. I wanted to hang onto my character, hang onto my culture, hang onto my identity and hang onto my status. So all of this was held onto, because my wife and I wanted it to last as long as it could. I think we were very mature in the mind as young Aboriginal people back then, to think like that.

CHAPTER 9

'Money Matters'

Money can make or break you
If you dare to allow it to
But it's mind over matter
That's what we need to do

Take better self-control
Of every cent we earn
And then invest it wisely
For financial good return

Resolve of money matters
With regard of any sum
Depends on money management
From our well-earned wage/income

This prominent personal provider
For our overall well being
Is our natural way of living
Like any human being

We indulge in mind and body
From the inside in on out
With fluid/food consumption
It's delicious there's no doubt

And we owe it to ourselves
To be happy anyway
If we spend a little extra
Don't fret, it's okay

Self-spoiling is a passion
A joy of one accord
But don't forget/remember
Only when you can afford

Its long been often said
And proven to be true
Money is the root of all evil
But there's goodness in it too

It's a powerful persuasion
Can be cruel, can be kind
It can clear our inner vision
Or leave us numb, deaf and blind

A remedial kind of cure
Like a double-bladed sword
A flashing bolt of lightning
Through our single life-line cord

*So be careful when we're counting
All our pennies in the bank
Make sure we've done our homework
Then give ourselves a vote of thanks*

*There's one more good old saying
Money doesn't grow on trees
But it's handy when we've got it
Just to put our minds at ease.*

By the time he was seventy-five, there was barely a club or hotel in Australia that Jimmy had not performed at. It was not only about the money for him; it was about the camaraderie and being a part of the upsurge of Australian music and taking others with him. For that reason, Jimmy did not think of himself as any more special than the others; it was just that he was less inhibited than most about getting up on the stage. He was definitely a lot more curious than most to find out what life would be like beyond the South Coast.

I would perform a lot with my fellow Aboriginal artists from Wallaga Lake, Batemans Bay, Moruya and Wollongong. We all performed around home in our singalongs and concerts and I was hoping at the time that some of the artists like myself would accompany me and come to Sydney. I told them a little bit about what I wanted to do, I said I wanted to make a record, but many were too reluctant to venture with me that far. But they kind of, in a way, wished me well; it was a big step for someone back then, and I'm not saying that I was anything special, it's just that I was keener than most to explore what was beyond what was then considered the borderline of going from community to mainstream. I didn't necessarily want to get away, but something inside of me kept saying, 'Greener pastures are somewhere just ahead,' and I was keen to explore that.

If you're happy, that's the main thing. It's not about finding happiness in being financially and materialistically successful in a foreign place; it's about being happy and successful in a familiar place, and that's the choice that a lot of my friends and family chose to make.

Before his 1963 hit with 'Royal Telephone', Jimmy had been able to use his success as a mainstream artist to support and promote other Aboriginal performers. One way he was able to do this was through his connections to Ted Quigg, which saw him touring with well-known Australian bands and singers in the mainstream.

Jimmy and Marj knew a lot of talented Aboriginal artists from their early days at the Waterloo Town Hall concerts, and Jimmy had worked in the timber yards in Mascot with several of the singers. When Jimmy put a few of them in touch with Ted Quigg, Quigg was only too happy to oblige and include them in shows he organised, partly because he believed in their talents but mostly because he could see it was marketable. Marj, however, would remain a little skeptical of the eagerness Quigg showed for putting together an all-Indigenous show, which would later be renamed the *All Coloured Show*.

The idea came about by myself and my [then] agent about the fact that it would be a novelty idea to put together a group of Indigenous star performers, including my brother Fred, who at the same time had his own shows happening – and would [go on to] be the MC compere of a regular venue in the suburb of Auburn, Sydney. The idea appealed to other theatrical agents and appealed to the club bookers. So the idea took off immediately, plus I had my own Indigenous band, so it was really an all Indigenous affair. Again, it was a plus, because there hadn't been a show of this nature, a show of this type or style, before, going around the entertainment industry. So it was a first for everyone concerned and very well received.

As well as his brother Fred, who was just as keen as Jimmy, and very talented, other people Quigg included in the all-Indigenous shows were people who already had their own emerging careers in the Sydney music scene, including Col Hardy, Noel Stanley, Clayton Davis, Bettie Fisher, Lorna Beulah and Jimmy's best man at his wedding, Claude Williams.

The disparity that divided Indigenous performers from the mainstream Australian music scene in the early 1960s was being addressed by Jimmy through his association with Ted Quigg, who would book the artists to play and tour cities and regional areas. Without overly worrying about the political implications, they were doing what they could to narrow the gap between Indigenous and non-Indigenous performers, and so it became typical for artists on both sides to be performing and touring with each other on the road, because it was the right thing to do, and it worked because they had talent.

They were fantastic times back then. When you think of the full houses at picture theatres and town halls and wintergarden theatres. They were just massive buildings that were full. Festival town halls

Frances Peters-Little

and every big dance hall you could think of at the time, they were just crowded with a wonderful audience that just gave us the greatest ovation and address and attention. Col and I, we just loved it all, and so did our co-stars in the names of Warren Williams, the Delltones, Barry Stanton, Jay Justin, Digger Revell, Judy Cannon, Vicki Forrest, Colin Cooper, Leo Reynolds and Rex Dallas. I just can't think of all their names, but certainly the people who remember that era will remember all those names and all those faces.

We'd travel the length and breadth of Australia. We toured from Tassie to the Top End in the Northern Territory, Adelaide, Melbourne. The only state I didn't get to in the days with Col was Western Australia. That came later with the Jimmy Little shows. But certainly, all the east coast and the Top End, and the bottom end, more times than once or twice, year to year, and all the bigger towns and some of the not so big towns that were stepping stones across the mileage that we travelled. Every town you can think of, like Bendigo, Warrnambool, Ballarat, Shepparton, and, talking about the southern parts, Port Pirie, Whyalla, Port Augusta, these places, and then Queensland, Rockhampton, Mackay, Townsville, Cairns. It was everywhere, everywhere you can imagine people would be. We did that more than once, so it was full on for all of us.

Also touring with them was Noelene Batley, who in 1961 was voted Australia's Top Female Singer; Lonnie Lee, who was a pioneer in Australian rockabilly music, with five gold records to his credit; the Dave Bridge Band, with Bridge acknowledged as Australia's top guitarist; and Judy Stone, who was Australia's leading pop and country music singer with several hits in the national music charts. Also appearing on stage on the tours was lap steel guitarist

Rob E. G., who rose to fame with his early hit '55 Days at Peking' (1963) and would produce three of Australian rock band Daddy Cool's albums, as well as producing albums for Marcia Hines, Air Supply, Tommy Emmanuel and flautist Jane Rutter.

Emerging from out of the Dave Bridge Band was guitarist Ray Burton, who went on to a very successful and distinguished career with a string of legendary Australian bands, including The Delltones, and was the co-writer with Helen Reddy of the international smash-hit 'I Am Woman'. Those with further claims to international fame during this period included Col Joye's brother Kevin Jacobsen (pianist for the Joy Boys), who ran his own entertainment agency. The agency had a string of Australian star power, including the Bee Gees, Olivia Newton-John and Little Pattie (aka Patricia Amphlett) of 1960s Australian 'surfer pop' fame. The agency was also responsible for bringing to Australia artists like Barbra Streisand, Barry Manilow and Sammy Davis Jr.

When the *All Coloured Show* began touring, Jimmy was not entirely comfortable with the name, but to be called 'coloured' in those days was seen to be more preferrable than being called 'Darkie' or 'Black', which were seen as negative terms in the 1960s.[109] This has become more acceptable since it was reappropriated by the Black Power movement in the United States, which, during the 1970s, espoused the concept that 'Black is Beautiful'. Ironically enough, the word 'Colour' has even made a comeback since the 1960s and is now used to describe 'People of Colour' (POC).

The *All Coloured Show* was made up of a mixture of individuals and families. Its aim was to introduce Aboriginal talents to mainstream audiences. For this reason, they sang popular songs that most Australians enjoyed. Candy Williams formed a duet with

Promotional poster for the *All Coloured Show*.

Jimmy's brother Freddy to perform the main musical comedy act of the show. It was a German folk song 'There's a Hole in my Bucket', which was recorded and made popular by Black American recording artists Odetta and (Caribbean singer) Harry Belafonte. Fred would dress up as Liza, and Candy played the role of Henry.

Jimmy and his brother Fred sang several popular tunes by Black American artists Sam Cooke and Jackie Wilson. When they performed together, Jimmy could see how Fred resembled their father Kunkus, with Jimmy being like his uncle Jack, the straight man. As well as their performances in the *All Coloured Show*, they continued to perform together every now and then.

Fred and I worked together a few times, not as an act, but whenever I appeared at his club as a guest, then we would perform a duet. At times when I'm somewhere performing, he would come along, and he would avail himself, and we would do a performance together. But the public got to know Fred as much as they knew me, and so we were always expected to perform as a duo whenever we were in the same room together. It was a nice impact, where [there was] two brothers with similar voices and similar, I guess, personality and family delivery; it was so easy for us and so natural. We should have done more, but we didn't get around to doing any more than we wanted to.

Sadly, some years later my brother passed away through an illness that suddenly took his life, and it saddened the whole music industry, because he was so likeable and so pleasant and so talented; he really was. He had more personality on stage than me. He was the court jester of show business, and I was the serious kind of stereotype.

The family groups associated with the *All Coloured Show* included Jimmy's brothers and sisters – Freddy, Betty, Monica and sometimes Colin – and the Opals, who were made up of singer/guitarist George Fisher and his sister Debbie on bass. Others included in the *All Coloured Show* were Matt and Clark Scott, who were cousins to the members of the Opals band. Rising to fame after leaving the *All Coloured Show*, George Fisher formed his own band, called Mr George, which played as support group for David Cassidy when he came to Australia, and released a single called 'So Much Love in My Heart', which hit the pop charts in April 1973, reaching number 23 in Brisbane, number 22 in Sydney and number 26 in Adelaide.

Some of the individual artists who were part of the *All Coloured Show* went on to have success beyond their existing singing careers. After her early days with the *All Coloured Show*, jazz singer Bettie Fisher (no relation to George Fisher), from the South Coast of New South Wales, became the administrator of the newly established Black Theatre Arts and Cultural Centre in 1974, which was based out of a Redfern warehouse. Candy Devine MBE, born Faye Ann Guivarra in about 1939 to a sugar-farming family in Cairns in Far North Queensland, had a multicultural heritage, with Sri Lankan, Filipino, Spanish, Danish and Torres Strait Islander backgrounds. She went on to become a radio broadcaster and singer in Northern Ireland, her career spanned over thirty-five years. Noel Stanley, who came from Narrandera, was another member of the *All Coloured Show*, and had a voice not unlike American yodeller Slim Whitman. Colin Hardy, from Brewarrina, was once dubbed the gentle giant of country-soul, and was the first Aboriginal person to win a Golden Guitar at Tamworth. Col recorded several albums, such as *Black Gold, Col Hardy – Country album, Black & White Tangle, Remember Me* and singles 'Protests' and 'Excuse Me'.

The *[All] Coloured Show* toured far and wide across New South Wales because of the clubs having poker machines. We didn't go too far beyond the borderline of New South Wales because of the clubs. Some of the artists were busily committed to day jobs, so they didn't have the freedom that I had to go for any length of time interstate.

Jimmy had hoped that they would all stay in the mainstream, and for a while he thought they were making inroads. One of the ongoing tasks for Quigg at that time, especially since there was no such thing as government funding for them in those days, was to secure funds and find sponsorship to get the 'show on the road', and he managed to do that a few times.

The happiest thing that I experienced with everybody was we were gaining recognition collectively as the First Australians and we were making an impression that was favourable in the climate of Aboriginal Australians still being kind of to the side of main events and not totally involved in mainstream community. That was creating a middle ground of getting to know how Aboriginal Australians operate, meaning how we conduct ourselves in predominantly non-Aboriginal society. There were a lot of public relations going on under the banner of entertainment. That was some of the joy that we found. We were making inroads, making good impressions, and creating conversation and a network of public relations across the board.

Despite their efforts, in the early 1970s the *All Coloured Show* began winding down, for a number of reasons.

The sad thing about that is we weren't all able to be together for as long a period as we all hoped. We had family commitments and we had other plans for our careers, and we wanted to stabilise the theme of it by recruiting new people, and we didn't have enough new people to recruit to keep the standard up. We had to then go back out into the single performing role of our lives. Candy would work differently. My brother became a stationary compere comedian at the Auburn RSL Club. This was fine. They were all working. Candy Devine went overseas, and Bettie Fisher was really busy with her commitments with Black Theatre. So we were all off in another direction.

The more Jimmy worked independently of the *All Coloured Show*, the more he needed his own band, and eventually he formed the second Jimmy Little Trio, composed entirely of Gamilaraay men.[110]

This Jimmy Little Trio consisted of Doug Peters on drums – my wife's younger brother from Walgett, who was recruited in the early days to be part of the band – Cyril Green, a guitarist from the township of Armidale, and bass guitarist Max Kim, also from Armidale.

Sadly, Max Kim suffered an illness which eventually took his life, and he was replaced by Neville Thorne from Walgett.

In 2005 Doug Peters, Cyril Green and Neville Thorne were awarded the Red Ochre Award from the Aboriginal and Torres Strait Islander Arts Board at the Australia Council for being part of the first Aboriginal band with a recording contract, and Doug and Cyril were both awarded an Order of Australia in 2011 for their contribution to the country music industry.

With its own musical style, the trio was described as 'very popular, straightforward, and traditional, which tended to differentiate [it] from other bands of the time'.[111] Cyril Green was considered to be one of Australia's first country musicians to popularise the so-called 'thumb style' of guitar picking, which was also used by Chet Atkins in Nashville.[112] Doug Peters, the drummer, learned Jimmy's style as he went along. The trio's first recording was *Jimmy Little Sings The Country and Western Greats* (1965) followed by *The Country Sound of Jimmy Little* (1969).

Although Doug and Cyril were the mainstay of the trio, Jimmy found he was always unlucky with bass players, who would move on for some reason or another. In the first Jimmy Little Trio, the bass players were Graham Tredennick, John McDonald and Stuart Kearney. Then came the second Jimmy Little Trio, in which the first bass player was Max Kim, then Neville Thorne, both of whom passed away. They were later followed by Jimmy Martin and Nelson Arentz, who were both Greek Australians – but in the interim there was Gary Williams, Neville Perkins, Gavin Flick and Stevie Lugnam – and finally came Tony Green. Tony was Cyril Green's son and stayed with the Jimmy Little Trio up until the end. The last performance of the Jimmy Little Trio was at the Jimmy Little's Memorial Concert at the Sydney Opera House, where the band supported Jimmy's grandson James Henry Little, who sang several of Jimmy's songs. For Jimmy, Doug and Cyril, the stalwarts of the second Jimmy Little Trio, always had a special place in his heart.

Jimmy Little and the Jimmy Little Trio. Neville Thorne, Cyril Green, Douglas Peters and Jimmy Little, 1963.

Dougie and Cyril and I, the three of us, we've just got some kind of a bond that has gotten stronger through the years, and we just grin when we think about seeing each other. When Cyril comes down, we say, 'Cyril's coming down to visit from Armidale' – and we have the biggest grin when we greet at the door, to be flooded in our memories and our thoughts of all those yesterdays. Doug, he lives pretty well next door to me, and even being that close and seeing each other often, we look at things on telly or we talk about early days, and we just can't help but laugh and joke about the good times and about all our band friends. It's something deeper than brotherly love somehow.

CHAPTER 10

'Who's to Say'

The good, the bad and the ugly
Who has the right to say?
Who is, what is and so on?
We hear things like this every day

It's a personal insulting observation
When thoughts are spoken out aloud
From colleagues with close-knit connections
And from strangers out there in the crowd

Though speaking our minds is understandable
There's really no need to be crude
When comments are so bad and ugly,
That's not good and just downright rude

I dislike all cruel accusations
From those with perfection in mind
When they sneer at other imperfections
In people with a complicated bind

Colour, height, size and impediments
Is no fault of the unlucky few
Who suffer these kinds of unpleasantries
From a biased cold attitude

Any kind of unwanted attention
Is crippling, sickening and unkind
When over the top criticism
Comes from an unsound mind

From birth we build an identity
Disregarding disabilities and such
Be it names, cultures and religion
To bear it all is often too much

But there is a deep seated reason
Why we cannot all be the same
Variety's a delicacy of spices
Like a ball we just bounce back again

Relish and cherish the moment
Of whom and what you really are
Damnation no match for admiration
So just follow your own guiding star.

When Jimmy wrote his poem 'Who's to Say', he could have been speaking about the prejudices some held against others, or he could equally have been referring to prejudices held against him. Jimmy hated intolerance and cruelty. He believed people should be taken on their own merits, not just the cultural background they came from, and thought that social trends were in constant progression; that what may be undesirable now might someday become acceptable or fashionable, or spin right back in reverse at any tick of the moment.

From the late 1950s into the 1960s and 1970s, Australia went through a tumultuous period politically. It was a particularly difficult time for Aboriginal people, who railed against the widespread assimilation policy.[113] With Jimmy's music career on a steady rise over this time, it seemed he was straddling two worlds – one as a mainstream Australian pop star, the other as an Aboriginal singer engaged in encouraging the careers of fellow Aboriginal and Islander singers and musicians who performed on the fringes of mainstream society. Although there were some who considered Jimmy Little to be sitting on the fence, he believed he was straddling the two worlds.[114] Jimmy felt that such views were mainly manifested by those in the media, and by people aligned with political groups. These critics suggested Jimmy had become too assimilated into White society and should have been more politically involved. Back then, Jimmy held to a dual view, saying, 'I have this in my focusing, I can see the stereo of life and I try to address both sides of the argument or the debate'.

Jimmy and Marj's response to their critics was to ignore them and continue on in the way their lives were headed, neither apologising for Jimmy's success nor for his unfairly perceived indifference. They also ignored those who held him back, and refused to back down. But what his critics were not aware of was that, from childhood, Jimmy had developed an attitude that allowed him to disregard those who thought of Aboriginal people as inferior and those who judged others unfairly, insisting that 'one must always treat ignorance with ignorance'.[115] It did not matter what side the 'ignorance' was coming from. Whether it was those who discriminated against him as an Aboriginal man, or whether it was his own people who expected him to be more politically outspoken. As his wife Marj said about political rallying and soapboxing, 'He's not a politician, he is an entertainer. What can he say politically other than just get out there and do it. But to take a soapbox out in the park somewhere and talk about things is not him. His politics started a long time ago.'[116]

What Jimmy and Marj felt they could do was to seek racial tolerance through music, and it was a conscious decision, as Jimmy's guitarist Cyril Green said:

> When we toured, especially with Jimmy, we were put on notice, we were expected to be on our best behaviour, because we knew if we played up, it would not reflect on us individually, but on our entire race of people, and Jimmy's reputation, as well as our own as Aboriginal people, so we went out in public all cool and stylish.[117]

At the height of his career, from the late 1960s to the early 1970s, Jimmy's patience would sometimes be tested by those who referred to him as a 'white man in black skin'.[118] Phrases Jimmy used – saying that he never felt disadvantaged, or that he could be anything he wanted to be – would, understandably, put people offside. But he was not making the statement that every Aboriginal person could be what they wanted to be; rather, he was saying that he thought he could be. And that was the difference – but that did not stop the accusation that he was a 'white man in black skin'.

The phrase 'white man in black skin' has a history that possibly goes back to the 1960s. It was aimed at Black people who were regarded as successful or accepted by the White mainstream. The origins of the term are unknown, but it was popularised in Hollywood and directed towards actors like Sidney Poitier for his performances in the films *Guess Who's Coming To Dinner* (1967) and *In The Heat Of The Night* (1967). These films conveyed the message that the central Black character was morally and culturally superior to the White characters in the films and that to be considered as an equal they would have to be 'superhuman'. In a similar vein, the term 'a man of black skin with a pure white heart' was used to describe Martin Luther King when he made his 'I Have A Dream' speech.[119] Other derivative terms like this have emerged from out of the archaic book by Harriet Beecher Stowe, *Uncle Tom's Cabin*, written in 1852, which led to the term 'Uncle Tom' being used to describe a Black person who 'sold out' his own people.

Closer to home, in Australia, the term 'Jackey Jackey' had its origins in a historical incident where supposedly a real person named Jackey Jackey (1833–1854) was the Aboriginal guide and companion to surveyor Edmund Kennedy, who ventured into Cape York Peninsula. This Aboriginal man may have been recognised by the colony of New South Wales, and his name engraved on a solid silver breastplate, but the term 'Jackey Jackey' implies a collaborator, a subservient 'native' complicit in his own people's dispossession, and thus a sell-out and traitor.[120] In later years, this term was replaced by 'coconut',[121] which was used to describe a Black person who conformed to White culture at the expense of his or her ancestral culture; it was closer to the adage 'white man in a black skin', implying that someone appears Black on the outside but is White on the inside. Criticisms such as these, in Australia, were aimed at successful Aboriginal people like Jimmy Little and opera singer Harold Blair.[122] There is an irony about this, because in those days, only a minority of Aboriginal people engaged in demonstrations and protest rallies. The vast majority of Aboriginal people, while maintaining a strong sense of Aboriginal identity, made a living for themselves working within mainstream society, with some leaving their Aboriginal communities behind to become financially secure as part of that mainstream society.[123]

It may have appeared from the media that all Aboriginal people were activists, but this was not the case. They were in the minority, but by the mid-sixties and late seventies they were receiving media attention. Jimmy's family had practised their own version of 'resistance' in their time, in their own way. His parents had participated in the Cummeragunja Walk-off in 1939, carrying him in their arms. His father had written protest songs, one of which Jimmy recorded.[124] His great-aunt, Jane Duren (1868–1947), wrote an appeal to King George V requesting the Aborigines Protection Board (APB) withdraw their control over the reserves they lived on as granted by Queen Victoria.[125] So it was not as though Jimmy had left his Aboriginal values and political beliefs behind him; rather, he had taken them with him into this 'new world', stating that 'politics has a place in all the things we do, as long as it's steady, on course and meaningful in the general community'.

It was not until 1958, twenty years after the Day of Mourning demonstration, that a group called the Federal Council for the Advancement of Aborigines (FCAA) was founded in South Australia. Later called the Federal Council for the Advancement of Aborigines and Torres Strait Islanders (FCAATSI), it became the first and most popular national body to represent Aboriginal and Islander interests.

It was FCAATSI that Jimmy became aligned with, along with people like Charles Perkins, Gordon Briscoe, Joyce Clague, Dulcie Flower, Faith Bandler, Bert Groves, Ken Brindle, Ray Peckham and others.[126] FCAATSI's aim was to achieve citizenship rights equal to those of other Australians for all Aboriginal and Torres Strait Islanders, and to establish living condition standards that were equivalent to those of other Australians. FCAATSI also sought equal pay for equal work for Aboriginal people, who, in many cases did not receive the same wages as White Australians, and it maintained a focus on claims to traditional land and cultural practices. While the Adelaide branch fought for the right to free and equal education, and for the right to retain the possession of all remaining native reserves, the Sydney branch wanted to get a referendum rolling, and after many years of hard work, this was achieved.

Up to this point there had never been a widespread media campaign such as the one led by Charlie Perkins with the Freedom Ride in 1965. Perkins (a founding member of FCAATSI's Adelaide branch) had been a somewhat lone Aboriginal voice, but in 1965 he became president of a group of Sydney University students who called themselves the Student Action for Aborigines (SAFA). They took their protests for civil rights for Aboriginal people on the road through regional New South Wales, challenging, for example, local authorities that banned Aboriginal children from the Moree and Kempsey swimming pools and segregation in the Bowraville and Walgett picture theatres, where ironically it was Jimmy's sister-in-law Marie Peters who was arrested for sitting upstairs in the Walgett picture theatre. Although the Freedom Ride did not directly change any laws, its greatest legacy is that it generated massive awareness about the struggle of Aboriginal people and their quest for equality and civil rights.

Also fighting for their land and civil rights was a group of approximately two hundred Aboriginal cattle workers who, in 1966, went on strike on Wave Hill Station in the Northern Territory to protest against their unequal work and pay in comparison to White employees, as well as the squalid living conditions to which they were subjected. They also demanded the return of, and the rights to own, a sizeable portion of their traditional lands.

The FCAATSI campaign to change the Australian Constitution continued until 1967. Then on 27 May 1967, Australians voted to include Aboriginal and Torres Strait Islander people as part of the population, allowing the federal government to oversee Aboriginal affairs. It was a landmark vote, with 90.7 per cent of Australians voting 'Yes' in their favour. The campaign strategy of the New South Wales branch of FCAATSI might have been naive, but it demonstrated how eager they were to encourage more Aboriginal people to move forward with White Australians 'hand in hand'. Jimmy, who always held out hope for the future, believed this could happen. As a follow up to the referendum, FCAATSI member Joyce Clague decided that Jimmy would appear in a short film urging Aboriginal people to get on to the electoral roll and act as equal citizens.

With the affairs of Aboriginal people making the news, particularly in 1965 and 1967, exposing numerous incidents of racism and segregation, it is interesting to consider why Jimmy's singing career was able to flourish even before all this. Naturally it became difficult for some to comprehend why on the one hand there was such low racial tolerance for Aboriginal people in Australia, yet on the other hand he was being idolised nationwide by White Australian audiences. Even more perplexing was why in 1962, a year before the release of 'Royal Telephone', and three years before the Freedom Ride, an all-Indigenous musical review was gaining popularity and being performed at venues that did not allow Aboriginal patronage. So perhaps the *All Coloured Show* was also able to niggle at White consciousness in some way or another, so that the racist managers and townsfolk would acquiesce on seeing that a younger generation admired and adored the Aboriginal stars. While it did not directly change all RSL clubs' policies on banning Aboriginal ex-servicemen from drinking at their bars, Jimmy still felt in his heart that sharing music and meeting people with a gently-gently approach was the best way to break down racial barriers. He did not think they needed to lecture others about the plights of Aboriginal people; he wanted to reach them on a human level.

To be face to face talking with an Aboriginal person from the community, and to know an individual who, from a distance, would have been something of a mystery; then when the mystery faded, and they spoke to another human being, with the same human feelings, the same needs and the same desires and ambition; when they realised that someone like me, at first, may have seemed so different to them, they might reflect on the rest of the Aboriginal community and say, 'Well, Jimmy is a representative of his people, and they might act and feel and operate the same way as him'. So if that could be a way of breaking down the barriers and bringing people together in an understanding way, then that's a good thing.

When Jimmy's hit single 'Royal Telephone' rocketed to the top of the music charts in 1964, and his success increased even further, Jimmy maintained that he wasn't being political, he was being artistic, and general entertainment was his program.[127] Jimmy was in hot demand, making multiple television appearances, gracing the pages of the mainstream magazines, and appearing at countless events and charity fundraisers. So how are we able to grasp the paradox? The only way that Jimmy could describe it was to say that in the end it was timing and talent; that Australia was at a coming of age, with its own Australian music industry, its own Australian identity. There were those who were scathing about Jimmy's rise to stardom, describing him as a novelty act, or as a 'poster boy' for a restrictive assimilation policy that, while it looked good on the surface, could only ever be achieved at the expense of the rights to have one's own Aboriginal identity, land, culture, language and customs. But Jimmy was able to shrug off such criticisms, saying that he was not to blame for the way others painted him. And when later he looked back over his life, he emphasised that he had been more than a novelty act, because novelty acts tend to wear off, but his 'act' lasted him a good fifty-five years in the industry.[128]

Whether such criticisms of Jimmy Little were truthful or not, they were immediately rejected by three of his friends at the time: Charlie Perkins, Bob McLeod and Gordon Briscoe, all of whom by then had high radical profiles. Perkins held Jimmy Little in great regard and acknowledged that both of them were fighting for justice and recognition – Jimmy through music and Charlie through politics.¹²⁹ Gordon Briscoe said that despite the criticisms, Jimmy 'never wavered' from his responsibilities and commitment to improving the affairs of Aboriginal people.¹³⁰ An even more revolutionary figure was activist and singer/songwriter Bob McLeod, who grew up with Jimmy in Woorigee, and said that Jimmy was only doing what they were all trying to do – get off the missions, get out in the bigger world and make a success of their lives.¹³¹

When Aboriginal issues started to appear in the news more frequently, Jimmy was called upon as a spokesperson. This was something he did not enjoy, but he felt that occasionally it was necessary. In 1967, when he appeared on 'Before the Referendum', on the ABC's *Monday Conference* program, he was not happy with the questions he was asked.

> I was getting a little annoyed with those questions coming time after time. I used to ignore what I called trivial, silly, childish questions, when I had a bigger plan and a bigger job to do – and I was going to get on with that job by saying if anybody small-minded thinks that I'm looking for fame and fortune in everyday mainstream society at the expense of my pride with my race and my humble beginnings ... so I tried to indicate to the people interviewing me that I wasn't going to be a victim of anyone's ignorance. That's why I said I treat ignorance with ignorance.

Jimmy had earlier been the presenter for an ABC documentary called *A Changing Race*, which aired in 1964. This was the first time an Aboriginal person had been chosen as presenter, and it was a ground-breaking film in that it presented the voices of Aboriginal people speaking directly about their concerns. Jimmy continued to maintain, though, that his music could make a greater difference than if he appeared as a political spokesperson.[132]

Unable to avoid being political altogether, Jimmy became president on the board of the Foundation for Aboriginal Affairs (FAA) in 1970. The FAA was formed in 1964, with Charlie Perkins, Ken Brindle, Reverend Ted Noffs and Bill Geddes as key founders. The aim of the FAA was to make contact with Aboriginal people moving to Sydney and help them to find jobs and housing. This would place Aboriginal people on an equal footing with other Australians, engaging them in social activities and helping them to achieve social inclusion and acceptance in mainstream society.[133] The FAA mostly raised its funds through donations, organising socials and selling Aboriginal artefacts and art from the Northern Territory and regional communities. While Jimmy was president, he was involved in the social activities and talent quests held to support fellow artists like the Silver Linings, Candy Williams and Max Silva. He also managed the busy coffee shop on George Street. The FAA eventually folded in 1977 due to a lack of funding and a general shift towards more grassroots organisations that were run by Aboriginal people.

Happy to have a break from the hustle of political action and committee meetings, Jimmy was keen to get back on the road again, and spent several weeks performing in remote Aboriginal communities and settlements in the Northern Territory. For Jimmy, the Aboriginal politics of the 1970s was going in a direction that was beyond his reach; he could see that the next generation of Aboriginal people, younger than himself, were justifiably angry, and that they differed from their Elders, who mostly lacked a formal education.

As I summed it up, this new generation were re-educated as young adults about the injustices that their parents and their grandparents got. So they said, 'No more. We want compensation, we want an apology, we want to start afresh on neutral ground for better rights and liberty.'

Jimmy thought this new generation of Aboriginal activists was unfairly branded by the media as irrational radicals, when all they were doing was standing up for their rights, and for the rights of other Aboriginal people. In his mind, they were fortunate enough to get an education and join other students and people across the world in rallies where they stood up for worthy causes. He was pleased to see them addressing past ill deeds, which needed to be recognised, because these ill deeds had been swept under the carpet for generations by people who were in powerful places and who did harm to Aboriginal people. He thought this new generation was able to express itself widely and internationally because these young people were highly articulate. He was glad that the actions they took became more widely accepted, although he did feel that at times they went about it the wrong way, which was hurtful to a lot of people.

In short, I congratulated the radicals, I supported them, but I felt that a lot of the non-Indigenous Australians didn't deserve to be painted with the one brush any more than all Aboriginal people were being painted with the one brush, but my Black brothers and sisters in the movement thought, 'You're either a part of the problem or part of the solution,' so it went straight down the middle.

It was important to Jimmy that someone could see the middle ground, and for a while during the early 1970s this was happening, with Aboriginal programs being set up that saw Black and White people working together.

He witnessed changes taking place in Sydney, and more specifically in Redfern – where he and Marj and their newborn baby lived in the late 1950s – with support in the early 1970s coming from non-Aboriginal people in the community such as doctors, lawyers, teachers and Christian organisations, rather than through government grants. At this time, the first Aboriginal legal service was established, as well as the first Aboriginal medical service, and the Black Theatre Company, in addition to an Aboriginal housing company and an Aboriginal-run childcare centre and preschool called Murawina, all based in Redfern. The driving force behind these services was the belief that 'Aboriginal people were the ones who best knew the problems of their people and they could solve their problems in the best possible way'.[134] It was a plan based on the rights of Aboriginal people to have self-determination.

Self-determination, for Aboriginal people, meant the right to have power over their own lives and self-governance of their own social, political, economic and cultural affairs. It meant having ownership of their traditional lands, and being able to resolve and develop their communities away from the paternalistic control of government departments that consistently controlled their funding and exerted authority over them.

By the late 1980s self-determination became more of a theory than a reality, as more Aboriginal services began to rely on government funding and the number of Aboriginal people working in government bureaucracies increased. This was a far cry from the days of the Aboriginal Tent Embassy that had been established on the lawns of Old Parliament House in Canberra, initially in 1972, and again in 1974, to protest for land rights.

Although he'd made a break away from politics, Jimmy still kept up his community engagements, and was a great supporter of Aboriginal football. He became the inaugural president of the Koori United team in 1974, after he was approached by a group of young Aboriginal men who were looking for a sponsor. Jimmy purchased their football guernseys, the colours of which he chose to be the same as his beloved Balmain Tigers team. Though the Koori United team no longer exists, the New South Wales Koori Rugby League Knockout carnival remains the largest Indigenous event in Australia.

In 1974 Jimmy also had a new hit country song, 'Baby Blue', which peaked at number eight in Melbourne and number thirty-seven in Sydney. As a result, his popularity with country music fans, many of them Aboriginal listeners, skyrocketed once again.

CHAPTER 11

'Four Seasons of Life'

Summer/autumn/winter/spring
A lifetime of learning to cope
Adjusting to all the elements
A treadmill of love/hate and hope

A journey of cross-road decisions
Go forward, go backwards or stay
Or maybe throw caution into the wind
Whatever will be, come what may

Destiny has her role to play
And so too does lady luck
Somewhere between two beauty queens
We manage to weave and duck

Three months in winter we hibernate
In mind, spirit and soul
Come summer we're out and about again
Some brash, some brave, some bold

Autumn comes at medium pace
Calm, collected and clear
Springtime plans again in place
To face another new year

Four seasons of fragrance and flavour
An abstract of shapes and design
A kaleidoscope look at the weather
Returning time after time

Summer/autumn/winter/spring
North/south/east and west
In spite of all adversities
Overtly we are blessed

This world of radiant colours
Illuminates in outer space
'Tis God's own global merry-go-round
Glowing in glory and grace

Our heavenly lord/creator
Has firmly put into place
The rhythm and rhyme of seasons in time
For the whole human race to embrace

Jimmy's 1974 hit song 'Baby Blue' was enough to sustain his career on the country music circuit, but its impact did not last long in the cities. Since his steady source of income came from the city audiences, he had to rely on his versatile tastes in music, and some of the connections he had previously made in the industry. It seemed that Jimmy's career was coming to a slow halt. As his poem 'Four Seasons of Life' suggests, by the 1980s Jimmy was learning how to adjust. He had reached a crossroads and needed to somehow break through. In parallel with the seasons, Jimmy was passing through autumn and knew winter was ahead. Many of his peers, who had hits during the 1960s and 1970s, were also now being overlooked for younger singers, who appealed to the younger audiences watching programs like *Countdown* on the ABC, and several others. The youth who once screamed at their pop idols on *Bandstand* had by now become parents or grandparents themselves and were settling back into quiet suburbia.

It was time to take care of his mind, body and spirit, and his family. He was in his forties and his recording contract with Festival Records had come to an end after his recording of 'Beautiful Woman' in 1983. Work in the nightclubs became increasingly difficult due to a recession that was putting pressure on the entertainment industry everywhere. Although he was able to find a steady stream of jobs and would perform at least once a week, it was not enough, and he could see that the clubs were beginning to cut back on live performances, replacing them with game shows, karaoke and bingo. Jimmy went through several managers, who 'all seemed to have great enthusiasm and vision for him, but they didn't have enough financial support and could not withstand the tough times nor the decline in the club industry'.[135]

Even though his wife Marj gave him emotional support, they often disagreed over the trustworthiness of new managers, and on more than one occasion she was right. The time came when Jimmy and Marj decided to do the managing for themselves, negotiating directly with booking agents and club managers, and their daughter handled press releases and marketing. As always Marj was the more wary one, while Jimmy wanted to believe the best in people. Even when they let him down, he would take a somewhat philosophical approach.

I can't glaringly pinpoint any such incident that made me too suspicious of their dealings. I just know that they were tough characters who sometimes 'robbed Paul to pay Peter', as the old saying goes. They did lots of juggling – and at the end of all that juggling of things, I never came out short.

To supplement the income he received from music, Jimmy grasped a new opportunity that came along in the form of part-time teaching. He was approached by well-known Aboriginal playwright Robert Merritt, who invited Jimmy to become a mentor and give inspirational talks to students studying performing arts. The Eora Centre was a college for Aboriginal students on Botany Street, Redfern, in those days. Jimmy arrived there just before it became part of TAFE and he watched as the Eora process unravelled.

> I was just a teacher, part-time, but I understood some of the politics and policy within the structure of Eora before it became part of TAFE. I understood that it wanted to be independent from TAFE control. But it got to the point where it needed to be restructured and re-established again. So to salvage the situation of not losing it altogether, they had to conform to the rules of TAFE, to become a recognised institution of learning.[136]

As far as Robert Merritt was concerned, it turned out to have been a stroke of genius to invite Jimmy there, because it transpired that Jimmy loved the work he was doing. He loved talking, philosophising and listening, and his students seemed to benefit from his mentorship. He never distinguished between who was an artist and who was not; to him, everyone was artistic and creative, and to think otherwise would be pretentious. Jimmy wanted to teach the students how to gain confidence, inspiring them to move into the mainstream, whether that was filmmaking, scriptwriting, television, poetry, acting, photography or working in the technical side of theatre, studying lighting and sound. He was actively engaged with his students, sharing knowledge and encouraging them. He would look directly at them when he spoke, preferably on a one-on-one basis, or would hang his head, staring at the floor, as he listened to them intently.

They'd tell me things that were happening in their community, and what's happening in their regions, so I'm getting lots of first-hand information on what's happening out there and how I may be able apply myself.

His time as a mentor at the Eora Centre had a lasting effect on him. It would be a learning experience that he would value greatly. He took much pride in watching his students develop, and wanted to know what might be holding them back. When they told him how much they wanted to break into the mainstream, Jimmy tried to help them understand what it meant for *him* to be in the mainstream. He could see that while they had the desire, they also wanted to remain in the community. He explained that they needed to identify a difference in their presentation between 'community' and 'mainstream'. This was ironic for him, as he had not had anyone that he could approach about being Aboriginal and moving into the mainstream; there had been no mentors or role models for him; he had trodden a path that was entirely of his own making.

Jimmy could see that times were different; unlike when he was starting out, Aboriginal students could now get support, and Aboriginal people in the arts were being supported through educational and government grants. He was happy they could get this support and was able to witness how mature the Australian public were becoming, willing to take in and value Aboriginal culture; in fact, it looked like they could not get enough of it. In watching the way younger Aboriginal people were willing to share their culture, and how much non-Aboriginal people consumed it, he reflected upon his own experience as an Aboriginal youth, when he grew up thinking that it was not his place to do that. When he was a younger man, he saw his father 'play act' Aboriginal culture, but they never discussed anything considered to be sacred or secret business publicly. To do so would have put the fear of Biame into them.

> If I can just touch on a point that for centuries our Elders didn't permit the younger warriors to present our culture, commercially speaking – our dance, our stories – everything about us. We were told not to use and abuse the rich cultural heritage that we had for commercial success – we don't have to give them the whole picture. But now it seems the floodgates have been opened, in terms of permission by the Elders – to say, 'All right,

young warriors and maidens, go and introduce us to the rest of the world. And so that's what's been happening.'[137]

Frequently Jimmy was asked why he had been able to 'walk through that invisible door' all those years ago, when other Aboriginal singers were not. Jimmy had never bothered to ask himself that question, but he assumed it was about having faith in his talent and being prepared to leave the South Coast and move to the city – with the encouragement of his father Kunkus. His students were putting him on the spot, expecting answers, telling him how hard it was for them to become successful. In response, he advised them that they needed to talk, dress and carry themselves in a manner that ensured they would not appear unprofessional. If they were going to enter a glamorous industry, they needed to have panache. His own view on why he was able to reach success was that when White audiences saw him, they were looking at someone who had more than just talent; they saw someone who stood out, and not someone who was trying to be White: 'I never wanted to be White in all my life; I just presented Jimmy Little, a shiny, glossy, natural and intelligent Black.'

He wanted the students to be aware of their own natural inner Aboriginal beauty, so that mainstream audiences would be drawn in rather than distracted or confronted by their Aboriginality. He said, 'People have to like you before they accept you, before they will listen, and when they accept you because they like you, even love you, then you deliver those natural goods you have inside.'

Jimmy was aware of himself as a Black man with an Aboriginal 'charm', and he understood that all Aboriginal people had it, but unfortunately they did not always know this. He was not interested in discussing racism and urged the students to do what he had done, which was to focus on their careers and goals, ignoring anyone who tried to hold them back or only treat them as a political issue.

He was acutely aware of the inequalities between Aboriginal and White people and never hesitated to talk about how he grew up in the depths of poverty during the 1930s and 1940s. He longed for a time when Black and White Australians might respect each other. When asked what White people could learn from Aboriginal people, he said, 'White people needed to erase in their minds any concept of what they thought a Black person is, because they had only been educated by other White people about every other race on the planet, and did not know any better.' He understood the value of finding more Aboriginal teachers who could find their own way and say, 'We're not a carbon copy of White activity; we are ourselves'. In his opinion, 'While White people might have more money and possessions than Aboriginal people, Aboriginal people held the greater knowledge and superior powers, because they could adapt to White law while holding onto their own communities, and maintaining their own rules, customs and traditions'. In addition to that, he was proud that they could excel in the White world despite the obstacles.[138]

Jimmy wanted to see a greater compromise between the two cultures, one where they could find a middle ground for negotiation. He hoped that a time would come when the media and so-called 'spokespeople' would stop making it difficult for the average Aboriginal people across Australia to live in successful family units, working things out between themselves. He made comparisons between Aboriginal and White people and the way they thought about equality.

The problem was that sometimes Aboriginal people and their cultural views about equality prevented them from becoming successful in the White man's world.

He hoped that White people could learn to be 'not so materialistic, and more family minded – develop a good sense of humour, like Aboriginal people, and try to be less uptight and serious'. Equally, he thought Aboriginal people might 'learn to take life a little more seriously, but not at the expense of their laidback ways, but more in the areas of finance and their health.'[139]

The Eora Centre provided Jimmy with the opportunity to talk about acting and the film industry. At that time, the Eora Centre became a hub for those looking for Aboriginal actors, and in each of their plays or films, there would always be a role for an Aboriginal male or female Elder, so Jimmy was often sought after. Still drawn to acting, he was an avid film buff, with an odd preference for vigilante films and gangster movies.[140] His favourites included *Manchurian Candidate* (1962), starring Frank Sinatra, and *Lawrence of Arabia* (1960), with Peter O'Toole. His favourite actors included Sean Connery (not so much for the James Bond movies but for later characters that he played), Gene Hackman, Ernest Borgnine, Lee Marvin, Kirk Douglas, Edward G. Robinson and Burt Lancaster.

In his first experience as an actor – when he played the role of Johnny the Stockboy in *Shadow of a Boomerang* – he shared a leading role with American actors Dickie Jones and Georgia Lee. This 'Christian Western' was inspired by Billy Graham's 1959 crusade – directed by Dick Ross, and written by Dick Ross and John Ford, it is about a cattle station manager who learns to overcome his prejudice against Johnny, the Aboriginal stockboy. Following that role, Jimmy had to wait another three years before returning to the big screen, in the 1962 film *Portrait of Australia*, and he wrote the music for and narrated another film, about the 'Chiller Trail' railway line, for BP.

Jimmy's early experience as a film actor taught him that, in many ways, acting was like singing, because it was about being able to interpret words and express them to an audience. Jimmy would frequently comment that he had always been an interpreter of words in his musical performances, so the transition to acting was not difficult.

In singing, one has to think about the musical tones, rhythm and musical instruments, and that is closely related to acting, insomuch as they are both about conveying a message, and interpretation, to the audience. As a singer, you get the immediate response of your audiences, and if you feel the time and mood is right, you can interact with them, by either talking to them, or directly making eye contact; so it's a spontaneous reaction. With theatre or film, the audience is invisible to you, and you have to rely upon your words and actions to reach them. You don't always know who your audience is going to be, so you cannot gauge them.

In both singing and acting, Jimmy felt the joy of knowing that he could give his best, serve his audiences, and leave them satisfied and energised, which is all that really matters. On stage, he appreciated the immediate response of theatre, whereas in film, he had to imagine how an audience, or a director, might respond.

I loved the audience listening intently and viewing you in a light situation of staging. And I loved the actors and actresses; we would be ourselves backstage, offstage, and then we would switch on to this character. That was exciting, to know somebody and then go on stage and be somebody else. It was a wonderful switch.

Jimmy's theatre-acting debut was in *Black Cockatoos*, written by Michelle Harrison and directed by Ned Manning. The play premiered at the Belvoir Street Theatre in Sydney in 1989.

The role I played was as an old man who lived by himself in the bush but became an Elder to this young man who was in some ways connected to my clan. The young man was in love with a non-Indigenous girl, and he used to ask me about how he will manage his tribal ways, having become attached to a non-Indigenous girl.

Then, in 1997, he appeared in Julie Janson's *Black Mary* as a duplicitous Black tracker. *Black Mary* was a story about an Aboriginal bushranger, Mary Ann, and her partner, Captain Thunderbolt, who roamed the north-western regions of New

Jimmy Little with actor John Blair on the set of *Black Cockatoos* at the Belvoir Street Theatre, Sydney, 1989.

South Wales in the mid-nineteenth century, and Jimmy's character was someone who turned against his own people, including Black Mary and Captain Thunderbolt. Ironically, Jimmy later found out about his wife being a descendant of Captain Thunderbolt and chuckled to himself whenever someone brought up about him playing the part of the person who sold out Thunderbolt and Black Mary to the police. The play was presented at the Wilson Street Carriage Works and was directed by Angela Chaplin.

The next feature film Jimmy appeared in was Wim Wenders's *Until the End of the World* (1991). He played the role of Peter, a tribal Aboriginal Elder in the central deserts of Australia, and a friend and half-brother to the character of Henry Farber, played by Max Von Sydow. The film is a science-fiction work set at the turn of the millennium in the shadow of a world-changing catastrophe. It also stars William Hurt, Solveig Dommartin, Sam Neill and Ernie Dingo. Jimmy was inspired by the range and calibre of actors in the film. Following the film, he and Max Von Sydow became friends in real life, and briefly exchanged friendly letters.

What I found was everyone turned me on stronger to my character. When I was with Sam Neill, I was delivering to him from his lead, and when I was with William Hurt, the character was just getting stronger and stronger. Max von Sydow, he and I were blood brothers from a traditional coming together ... Justine Saunders, Ernie Dingo, David Gulpilil, Bart Willoughby, Rhoda Roberts, everyone gave me a boost in my character, because our dialogue together was meaningful all the way through ... I was able to build on my character because of the words delivered, the dialogue delivered to me, and then I had to respond.

In 1993 he acted in a film called *Black River* alongside Maroochy Barambah and Russell Page. This musical drama was based on the story of a young woman whose son was killed in police custody.[141] Jimmy's part in the film was as the father of the young man killed by police. In 1999 he appeared in Paul Fenech's *Somewhere into the Darkness*. In this film he played the role of an Aboriginal Elder who foresees the events leading to the collapse of a building, in which a young boy and an old Irishman become trapped.[142]

Jimmy didn't perform in any further films or plays, but said that if he had been given the choice, he would have done more.

As far as Jimmy's singing was concerned, even though he insisted that 'he felt he was a mix of many flavours of music', there is no doubt that country music was his favourite, and that was the genre that people wanted to pin him down to. Jimmy did not mind that he was often labelled an urban cowboy singer, as the long association he had with country music echoed his rural background, of which he was very proud.

It was like folk, storytelling songs in the country flavour, and I took that with me to the city. In some ways, I was termed the urban cowboy, whereas we associate cowboys with cattle and sheep and farm work, and all that kind of thing. So here I am telling these stories in song to the city slickers, and me becoming a city slicker myself. So it was a nice mix of the urban cowboy singing in this style for the many, many people from all walks of life and from all backgrounds.

Jimmy, the urban cowboy, attended the Tamworth Country Music Festival almost every year, including the very first time the festival was staged, in the Tamworth Town Hall in 1973. In his last appearance at the festival, in 2011, he received his first Golden Guitar award. He was bestowed other honours at Tamworth, such as being inducted into the Hands of Fame in 1978 and having a life-size model placed on display in the Gallery of Stars Wax Museum the same year. He also enjoyed offering his support at the Aboriginal Cultural Showcase (with people like Roger Knox, who gave so much to Aboriginal country music), which was created by Aboriginal country singers to celebrate and promote Aboriginal and Torres Strait Islander country performers during the week-long Tamworth Country Music Festival.

When he could not go to Tamworth, Jimmy maintained his ties to his country music fans through the Brian Young country music tours. The first one was held in 1988 and the next was in 1991. These tours involved singers and bands being flown in small aircraft across no less than 35,000 kilometres of outback Australia, to communities that were remote and poor, many of them Aboriginal communities.

You had your own tuckerbox; you had your own swag for camping; and you had your own little place to enjoy the scenery, travelling out to outstations and to the smaller towns and the remote areas. To do that day to day – on my first trip, it was flying everywhere. That was one-night stands, flying by charter, small aircraft – and all the luggage and the rest of the band and the other artists ... You just had a different place every night, different people, and the same unit to work with, so it was really comfortable, and exciting. I loved that, and I did that the second time around by four-wheel drive.

A poster for one of Jimmy Little's appearances on the Brian Young country music show. This poster is from Jimmy's personal scrapbook and is signed by his co-stars.

Following on from Jimmy's time working with the Eora Centre, Carole Johnson, a dancer and graduate from the Alvin Ailey dance academy in New York, invited Jimmy to be a director for the National Aboriginal and Islander Skills Development Association (NAISDA); some of its early claims to fame included having Stephen Page and Christine Anu as graduates of the school. While there, Jimmy was appointed to the board of the Fifth Festival of Pacific Arts, which was held in Townsville in Queensland. It would be the first time the Festival of Pacific Arts was held on Australian soil, and the position allowed him to work and travel in the Cook Islands, Samoa, Tahiti and New Zealand; he was now considered to be an 'Elder' and people began calling him 'Uncle'.

The Fifth Festival of Pacific Arts, which was held in Townsville, involved over twenty-two different nations participating, from as far as Hawaii, Tahiti, and all over the Pacific. I was a delegate on a tour designing that, as artistic adviser. So that was a great experience. I had ten, eleven months' involvement in helping to program that.

As the 1980s rolled into the 1990s, Jimmy began facing new challenges in his personal life: 'The 1980s were a trying time for the Little family. For me personally it was a trying time, and very tough.'[143] At this stage, their daughter Frances, who grew up strongly influenced by the Australian Women's Liberation Movement, was raising a baby at home with her parents. If Jimmy and Marj ever wished they could persuade their feminist daughter to settle down and find a nice man, they never told her about it. Instead, they encouraged her to go on to university, which is exactly what she did: 'My daughter, as a career woman, didn't want to marry. And she wanted to have her son reared by her mum and dad, as the best people in the world to rear him in a single-parent situation. And we wouldn't have it any other way.' When his daughter asked him if he was embarrassed about her being a single mother, Jimmy replied, 'Men have sex with women out of wedlock all the time, so what you did was natural, and as a result you are going to bring a beautiful baby to the family'.[144]

Jimmy and Marj raised James the same way they had raised their own daughter. They idolised their grandson, taking him on the road with them when they travelled, teaching him more about the world and encouraging him to take to the stage like Jimmy and his siblings. On completing her university degree, Frances began work as a television researcher at the ABC, and she held a shift on the community radio station Radio Redfern, 88.9FM. One of the projects she worked on was a music clip for her father's version of the Toots and the Maytals reggae track 'Beautiful Woman'. Not surprisingly, the song received a lot of airplay at Radio Redfern in Sydney, so when it came time to do the video clip, there were plenty of extras making themselves available.

'Beautiful Woman' was a reggae single. It was on the flip side of [my version of] Bob Marley's 'Is This Love?'. A music clip was made for 'Beautiful Woman' that was organised by my daughter Frances with ABC TV, which was appreciated by many people, particularly Indigenous, because, in the music clip, I featured a lot of pretty ladies, faces from the Aboriginal Medical Service in Redfern, full on the screen as I sing. And they danced with the students from the National Aboriginal and Islander Dance Academy in Glebe.

This was an era when, resonating with his poem at the beginning of this chapter, all four seasons came at once for Jimmy. With so much going on, something would have to give, and that turned out to be Jimmy and Marj's health. Jimmy's blood pressure became a concern, fluctuating from high to low, and the debilitating asthma with which Marj had been diagnosed in 1958 worsened, as did the diabetes she had contracted when in her forties.

Jimmy missed singing and touring – it was what he loved most – but it was becoming increasingly difficult to find the work, and he slumped into a depression. By the mid-1990s, there were times when Jimmy and Marj thought they may need just to give in, and that Jimmy should stop singing altogether, but they decided against going down that route and thought they should stay strong as a family unit.

Part of the bonding and part of the ties that bind for Marj and I were our two children. One was an adult already and the other one was still at school, so we didn't want to let either one down by throwing our arms up and saying, 'Well, the industry's gone sour. We're going to pull up stakes and move on.' It entered our minds, but it never stayed in our minds for long. We had to readjust to the budget, and that was a little strange and a little tough for a while, but we knew there was a light at the end of the tunnel.

As it turned out, the light at the end of the tunnel came in the form of an unexpected new connection.

CHAPTER 12

'Reincarnation'

Everything in life is recycled
We all return to live another day
Life and death is just another timeframe
With the new and different roles we have to play

The journey from beginning without end
Is a mixture of pleasure and pain
We each get our chance to serve a purpose
When called upon to do it all again

We don't always re-appear as humans
From the waiting room where we get to choose
But one thing for sure we won't remember
When our past life is restored and renewed

There's another important factor for our being
Some are here to inspire and to lead
Masses of the free-thinking people
Throughout all phases of life's expectancy

History's full of legendary heroes
Of kings, martyrs and saints
They come to lead in silver-shining armour
Disregarding any fortune, fame or fate

I too suspect I've lived other lifetimes
I also believe there is a heaven and hell
With peril for the sad and forsaken
And with praise for those who had done well

Being good, being bad, or indifferent
Is no guarantee that life will treat you fair
So just read through the script you've been given
Then take weight of the cross you'll need to bear

We need to experience all the elements
To clarify between right and wrong
Our lifespan is an unforeseen closure
All we do know is one day we'll be gone

But like I said there is no real finale
To life here on earth or beyond
It's a continuous/conscientious journey
Embrace it as you would a life-time bond.

In June 1996, Jimmy Little performed at the Lyric, a short-lived music venue in Darlinghurst's Little Italy, in Sydney, on the inaugural occasion of a new monthly Indigenous music night organised by Bob Maza. Jimmy sang a few songs upfront to kick the night off. They included the evergreens 'Tie a Yellow Ribbon' and 'The Shadow of the Boomerang'. Australian producer, singer, songwriter, composer, author and performer Brendan Gallagher was in the audience and described Jimmy's performance.

> I arrived just as he began his set. He was utterly captivating, exuding a genuine warmth from the stage, real star power, and he had the most beautiful voice. I just thought he was one of the best singers I'd ever heard. I knew who he was, because I was five or six years old when his signature hit 'Royal Telephone' was being played everywhere in the early 1960s. But I actually thought he had died, just hadn't heard of him for such a long time.[145]

After the show, Gallagher introduced himself to Jimmy, who recalls that meeting.

After I came off stage, Brendan Gallagher came up and introduced himself. He said, 'Jimmy Little, you're a legend'. He asked me what I was doing music-wise and I replied not much. He asked would I be interested in talking about doing something with him and I said sure and gave him my phone number.

Gallagher called Jimmy a few days later to say he had a proposal. When he visited Jimmy and Marj, it was a pleasant surprise to realise that he had been at university with their daughter Frances. Gallagher's proposal was to reinterpret some well-known Australian songs in a new and different way, with a great and established singer (that is, Jimmy Little). At that stage, Gallagher had two songs in mind, 'Quasimodo's Dream' by The Reels, and 'Down Below' by The Cruel Sea, with a view to record more songs on an album of unique interpretations. The deal was simple: Jimmy would bring his voice, and Gallagher would do the rest, a fifty-fifty venture.

At first Brendan indicated that it was kind of experimental, and I was willing to go along with that to see how far I could extend myself. He wanted me to cover 'Quasimodo's Dream' [written by Dave Mason and released by The Reels in 1981] with a change from 4/4 time to 6/8, like a waltz, spacious and moody.

This meeting took place at a time when Australian politics was turning ugly. Senator Pauline Hanson had just been elected to federal parliament on a racist platform. Gallagher was hoping to do something positive in terms of reconciliation – an older and wiser Blackfella (Jimmy Little) working on a project with a younger Whitefella (Gallagher) to do something positive together. The project was primarily about making a great record, but the symbolism was not lost on the two men, with Jimmy and Brendan not only bridging the gap between Black and White Australians but also younger and older music fans.

The obvious bridge was to get across to a younger generation and the bridge was Brendan Gallagher.

In July 1996 this became a fruitful working relationship. Jimmy would go over to Brendan's studio in North Bondi and, over a pot of tea, they would listen to songs and discuss what could be done with them: what key, tempo, and so on. When they agreed on numbers, Brendan played the guitar and Jimmy sang the songs. This was in the early days of the internet and CD technology. A variety of songs were thrown into the mix – Australian Crawl's 'Reckless' and 'Downhearted', AC/DC's 'Long Way to the Top', and an idea to reinterpret Midnight Oil's 'Wedding Cake Island', with Jimmy reciting a poem by Oodgeroo Noonuccal/Kath Walker over the top. All sorts of people suggested all sorts of songs, and everything went into the sonic blender to see what came out.

It's like the artist that is trying to explain something – like a child might use their hands, and they can try to show us but can't. But they can see the end product while they're doing it. It's like when we're performing a song and we get up and sing it and feel if the audience has understood it.

The only song Jimmy was familiar with was 'Blackfella/Whitefella' by the Warumpi Band. His head had been in another songbook and he was happy for Gallagher to throw songs at him. Jimmy would stand in between the stereo speakers with his eyes closed, listening intently to a song, and at the end, he'd say, 'Play it again, Bren'. He had a tenacious work ethic; he would chase a song down.

I wanted to complement the writers and get that across. I'd listen to the singer and then I'd put them aside for the moment. I didn't want to imitate them.

Gallagher had a Tascam 38 1/2" tape machine (later two DA 88 digital tape machines) and a Seck mixing console, some mics, guitars, an accordion, bouzouki, mandolin, assorted drums and percussion, and an old upright piano. He recorded the 'Quasimodo's Dream' bed track in his lounge room on acoustic guitar with Michael Quigley (drums) and Michael Galeazzi (double bass). The 'Down Below' bed was recorded on a 12-string acoustic guitar, with Stuart Eadie on kettle drum and percussion. Jimmy came over a couple of weeks later and recorded his vocals. As Brendan Gallagher recalls:

> That's how all the *Messenger* tracks were done. The only recording that was made off-site was a one-off session at the Festival Records studio in Pyrmont, where they recorded Stu Hunter playing keys on 'Cattle and Cane', 'Alone With You' and ['Are You] The One I've Been Waiting For?', and Paul Hester [Crowded House] playing brushes on 'Cattle and Cane', recorded in a hallway out the back of the Gershwin Room [at the] Esplanade Hotel in Melbourne, where the *Rockwiz* TV show was taped. Everything else, drums, brass, strings, vocals, were all done in my flat.[146]

By design, Gallagher had a lot of different people playing on the record. He wanted it to be an homage from musicians and songwriters of another generation to a great Australian singer. He pulled in favours from all over and either paid musicians or swapped a guitar recording session with them. The fee was the same for everybody, a modest one hundred dollars. By the time they finished recording, in early 1999, more than two dozen musicians had contributed to *Messenger*. Marj recalled how she felt about this new record of Jimmy's.

> When Jimmy first brought the tape home, I said, 'What are you doing?', and he said, 'I got the tape here, have a listen'. So, I played it, I whizzed it on, and I whizzed it off, and I said, 'Nah.' But I played about five more songs, and I put it aside and I said, 'You're not doing that, are you?' But he said, 'I think it sounds okay,' then I said, 'But that's not you'. But it proved me wrong, didn't it?[147]

The album wasn't originally called *Messenger*. Its working title over the years of recording was *The Jimmy Little Experience*. After two years of trying to sell their work to record companies, they finally signed a deal in 1998 with Festival Records, the company Jimmy had signed with back in the 1960s. Then they had to promote it. For the launch of *Messenger*, Jimmy bought a white suit with white shoes, and he threw himself into his rejuvenated career, which ultimately took him all over Australia as well as abroad (Germany, the United Kingdom and the United States).

> The night of the launch of the album at the Embassy nightclub in Double Bay, I hadn't been so flamboyantly dressed for such a long time. And I felt like such a new superstar from out of 'somewhere' – I don't know where, but somewhere. And it was a wonderful release, a release of energy.[148]

Messenger remained popular and Jimmy was in big demand to perform live, so Gallagher's band, Karma County, was drafted to back him until he could put together his own crew. Graham

'Buzz' Bidstrup was at the launch party for *Messenger*, where he was asked about taking on Jimmy as an artist and booking him through his agency (Buzz Management). The first gig he booked for him was the Queenscliff Music Festival, on the Bellarine Peninsula, near Geelong, where Jimmy performed solo (guitar and vocal), appearing with Archie Roach and others. Jimmy knocked it out of the park and the festival organisers immediately booked him for the following year. However, they wanted him with a band, so a band would have to be put together, and the obvious choice was Karma County along with other musicians who played on the album. Later on, Buzz Bidstrup put together another band, again with some of the musicians who had played on the album.

At one of these performances, at the Hoey (as the Hopetoun Hotel was fondly nicknamed), Marj came to the show and sat in the front row in a big comfortable chair. She was not all that keen on the songs at first, but slowly she came around to the 'new' Jimmy.

At the Hoey, the place was packed, standing room only, and the age group of the audience was younger than usual for a Jimmy Little show. At the end of the first song ('Under The Milky Way'), when the last note faded, there was an almighty roar from the crowd. Jimmy, initially caught off guard by the reaction, grew a couple of inches taller. He turned around to the band, beaming, and then he really started to work the crowd. He was back![149]

> It was like I was reborn into the music industry. So, after three years of getting that record together and finally having it there in the package and presenting it, that was such a high for me. It was like shedding old skin and becoming a new me.[150]

Jimmy at the launch of *Messenger* with Melinda and Sean Kennedy, Costa Georgiadis, Brendan and Lee-Anne Gallagher. Double Bay, 1999.

Jimmy's message was to spread the love, and he did. A year before the album was released, Jimmy told filmmaker and writer Robin Hughes:

> To me, music is a message, like a message stick or a smoke signal or an important document. So when I'm singing songs it's like breathing life into [them] and conveying a message, and I see myself as a vessel delivering a message. So I'm speaking to my audience. I'm singing, but I'm speaking to them in a sense.[151]

People never forgot being in an audience when he performed, or being one-on-one with him, when suddenly they felt like they were the only person in the room. He made you feel good, and you never forgot it.

Recording a large string session one time for a post-*Messenger* project, two of the young violinists reported how excited their grandmothers were that their grandsons were playing on a Jimmy Little record. Brendan Gallagher recalls that touring with Jimmy was an education.

> Watching him make an entrance, read the crowd,
> create his own ambience, sometimes send us off for
> our 'lemonade break', whatever it took to entertain his
> audience. He loved to win a crowd, and he always did.
> We learnt so many songs on stage, whatever it took, and
> we had to follow him. Many times afterwards, sitting
> backstage after a show, I'd say 'Great show tonight,
> Jimmy,' and he would invariably reply, 'Almost as good as
> the Hoey, Bren, almost as good as the Hoey.'[152]

On tour, Jimmy handled downtime, the enemy of all performing artists, extremely well. He had the great gift of being able to power down completely, enter a trance-like state, for hours sometimes. And then, like something in nature responding to a subtle change in the atmosphere, he would emerge from his torpor, put on his stage clothes, do his hair and be ready for showtime.

When I need to escape, I shut down from the world around me, I close my eyes and I dream. And music accompanied [me] in my dreams. And music is a way to take me there and bring me back.

Friends and colleagues observed how Jimmy Little had the capacity to be either invisible or the centre of attention. He always won over the crowd and had the resources to equal the demands of any occasion. When he walked on stage, he was completely open, hands at his side, palms out, his smile welcoming, and those big liquid brown eyes telegraphing an assured sweetness. The audience was already his. Jimmy would summon all the magic in a room and take his adoring public out of themselves to somewhere quite beautiful. He could 'wow' any audience, anywhere, anytime. And he did this for fifty-five years.[153]

It was Jimmy's longevity and versatility in the industry that always inspired other emerging artists, especially Aboriginal artists. He told Leah Purcell – Aboriginal actress, director and writer, and winner of a Helpmann award – that to be able to walk onto the stage at his age, sing all those contemporary songs, look into the audience and see his old fans as well as new ones, was gratifying. She replied that the sad thing about his return to the stage was that, in the eyes of Indigenous people, Jimmy had never gone away.[154]

Rock historian and journalist Glenn A. Baker said of him:

The idea that young musicians would come along and pay homage to him, and he would re-establish his career is just wonderful. And without that he would have just had his niche and he would have continued in that niche, and not have the attention that he had with *Messenger* and what it brought.[155]

The *Messenger* album had an impact on many levels. It exposed younger Australians to a living national treasure in their midst, recast great songs in a new light, and introduced the music canon of an older generation to a younger one.

In a follow up to *Messenger*, Jimmy recorded his *Resonate* album, which was released in October 2001. The songs collected were again written by Australian artists. There were songs written by Paul Kelly, Don Walker, Bernard Fanning, Mark Callaghan, Brendan Gallagher and Dave Mason, and one track was co-written by his daughter Frances with the album's producer, Daniel Denholm, who co-produced the album with Brendan Gallagher and Richard Pleasance. Reviews for *Resonate* – which was very much unappreciated and underplayed – came in from listeners from the United Kingdom to the United States, stating that *Resonate* was so underrated. The reviews spoke of how the warmth in Jimmy Little's honeyed, lightly warbling voice, as it winds its way deep into your comfort zone, had been well hidden, despite Jimmy having been around forever; and that at some sixty odd years, he could still manage to send tingles up the back of your neck with the slightest of ease: 'Special stuff indeed. The man is a legend.'

A country album called *Down The Road* followed on from *Resonate*. Produced by Buzz Bidstrup, Marty Hailey and Mark O'Connor, it was released in 2003. On the album, Jimmy sang three duets: with Troy Cassar-Daley, Melinda Schneider and his grandson James Henry. Australian musician David Temby's review of this album described how hearing the tracks on *Down The Road* helped someone like him, who was not familiar with Jimmy Little, to understand why so many held him in such high esteem.

The next album, which was released in 2004, was *Life's What You Make It*, once again produced by Brendan Gallagher. Brendan and Jimmy wanted to record an album of popular songs that would be spiritually inspirational. With this album, they wanted to send a positive message to the world. Brendan thought of it as a faux gospel style record of non-gospel songs. The album featured songs recorded by popular overseas artists such as the Red Hot Chilli Peppers, Neil Young, PJ Harvey, Brian Wilson, Bruce Springsteen and Ben E. King, and many more. Brendan describes the driving force behind the album.

Life's What You Make It had a political undercurrent. The invasion of Iraq was the backdrop for the album's genesis and, as I explained to Jimmy, the world was hurting and needed a healing voice, and his was it. Such lofty themes are very rarely discerned by the listener but for an artist it is the secret mission, the in joke, that sustains the process.[156]

A series of compilation albums came next, such as *Passage* (2002) and *The Definitive Collection* (2004). And these would not be the last Jimmy Little albums to be released. *Treasure: The Very Best of Jimmy Little* (2012), *Songman* (2013) – a three CD special edition album, which featured *Messenger*, *Life's What You Make It* and *Live At The Studio, Sydney Opera House 2001* – and *At Last* (2013) would be released following Jimmy's death.

After *Messenger* came out in 1999, Jimmy also recorded a number of duets, often with well-known artists, such as 'Bury Me Deep In Love' with Kylie Minogue, 'Happy Day' with Olivia Newton-John, 'I Remember' with Kate Ceberano, 'Reach Out' with Melinda Schneider, 'Baby Blue' with Warren H. Williams, 'Holding You' with Jean Stafford, 'This Ancient Land' with John Williamson, and, with his grandson James Henry, 'A Reason For It All'. By 2006, though, Festival/Mushroom Records had begun to unravel and the company found itself in financial dire straits, selling off its assets to Warner Music Australasia, who currently distributes his music.

When the resurgence of Jimmy's musical career was at its height, a close friend of Brendan Gallagher's made a documentary film about Jimmy. Brendan's friend, Sean Kennedy, wrote and directed a one-hour documentary called *Jimmy Little's Gentle Journey*, telling the story of how Jimmy, as a pioneering artist, defied incredible odds to tread a gentle path of love and humanity through music. The film was shot over a period of several years but finally went to air on the ABC in 2003. The film, which was warmly welcomed by the Little family, features interviews with Jimmy, Marj, Frances and James. *Jimmy Little's Gentle Journey* remains as the most intimate and comprehensive biographical portrait of Jimmy's life. And as it happens, as well as Brendan Gallagher and Sean Kennedy, the film's producers, Frank Haines and Simeon Bryan (also cinematographer), all went to university with Jimmy's daughter Frances fifteen years earlier.

At the end of this book, the reader will find a discography of Jimmy's record releases.

CHAPTER 13

'Guided by His Love'

I'm just a pen in the hand of my Lord
A chisel meant only to carve
I'm just a voice to whisper his words
To help calm some restless heart

I'm just a needle to help stitch and sew
The fabric of lives torn apart
One single prayer will help you there
What you need to do is start

I can be found in the kitchen
A utensil ready at hand
Just take a look at his recipe book
'Cause I'm your pots and pan

I'm also out there in the garden
A tap, a hose, a rake
A spade, pruner and trimmer
Whichever tool it takes

I'm just a paddle for rowing the boat
Across the river of life
I'm just a whistle or bell to ring
For those without vision or sight

I'm just a torch, a glow in the dark
For finding a way through the night
His target in view for those that do
Need guidance from trouble and strife

I am a key to unlock the door
To window his light coming in
His promise of peace that will never cease
While-ever we listen to him

Whatever I am or am willing to be
I'm here at my master's request
All I can do is follow his cue
And give of my all, my best.

Many people have tried to pin Jimmy Little down on his spiritual beliefs. At times, this brought him popularity, but at other times, criticism. Some people have claimed that his Christian beliefs were a failing because they caused him to turn his back on his Aboriginal culture. They said he was extremely naive not to recognise the damage Christianity had done to Aboriginal people. Jimmy's earliest years were spent on a mission at Cummeragunja, where, along with hundreds of Aboriginal people of his generation and the generation before that, he attended the Church of Christ. Like them, he was always able to link Aboriginal spiritual beliefs to what he was taught at Sunday School.

> I would say at the age of six and seven at Sunday School on the mission settlement, I was always interested in stories and journeys of people. And so when they told us about different creation Bible stories and passages, and sang, music was involved, so I was into that anyway. And with my Aboriginal learnings about Mother Nature, it answered a question within me about who made them. And the force that made the universe made all of us. So I linked that all up then about how important Christianity was.[157]

Mixed in with those learnings, Jimmy also believed, to a degree, in reincarnation. He felt he had been here before and that the lives of all beings were cyclic. He thought he had been a woodsman in a previous life and that in the future he might reconnect with his traditional totems, which were the long-neck turtle and black duck. A journalist once wrote that Jimmy was thinking of leaving singing behind and becoming a man of the cloth, but Jimmy denied this, saying he thought the journalist had misunderstood him and that his plan was to reach others through music, and that was all.

Whatever his beliefs were, he was always known as a kind person who wanted to help others. He was uncomfortable about receiving help himself, but he saw a lot of pain in the world and leaned on his faith as a way of helping others. He spoke about belonging to a human family, which was his extended family, and he spoke about the enemies we share in common, such as hunger, cold, sicknesses or heartbreak. He expressed how he felt helpless much of the time and wanted to ease that pain, but had to learn how to choose between those things he could improve and those things he had to let go of.

There were aspects of himself that made him deeply angry, although he never really showed this to anyone.

> There's two people inside of Jimmy Little: the public and the private. And the private person takes the anger on the inside, and it subsides over a period of, really, moments, maybe days. So, in other words, I keep that to myself. I don't make that public, because it's my hurt. There's no reason why I should go out and cry on their shoulder. To me, then, it seems like looking for self-pity. And while I'm deeply emotional, I would rather take my own hurts and disappointments on the inside and deal with them personally until it's all at a comfort zone where, all right, I've dealt with that now.[158]

The things that made him the angriest were cruelty and domestic violence, especially the violence his sisters Betty and Monica suffered – but which they never shared with any of their brothers, Colin, Freddy or Jimmy. Later on, the boys saw the damage that had been done to their sisters and felt powerless to be able to help them.

> I'm really angry with domestic violence. It's been in my family. My sisters suffered domestic violence. I was not on the ringside, I didn't see it, but I saw the end results of it.[159]

As a younger man, Jimmy did his best to help strangers through his charity work, but recognition for his lifelong quiet dedication to helping others was not publicly acknowledged until much later in his life. The first award he received, which surprised both Jimmy and Marj, was in 1989, when he was a recipient of the National Aborigines and Islanders Day of Observance Committee (otherwise known as NAIDOC) Aboriginal of the Year Award. In 1997 he received the John Campbell Fellowship Mo Award for an outstanding contribution to the community beyond his normal career in the entertainment industry. Then came a swag of awards following the release of the *Messenger* album, which seemed to remind people that he was still around and active in the community.

Jimmy's opinion about receiving awards was that they were not a priority, but he was able to appreciate the honour and lifetime acknowledgements that were paid to him, and he graciously accepted them.

> That's why awards are so important. Your life being well documented in print and in films and photographs, and word of mouth – all these things never go away and leave you. They're there for people to remember, because it's important to be able to make that contact with the public, and the people in between the public. So I don't fear the day that I will feel I've had my turn, now it's somebody else's.[160]

In 2002 Jimmy was named New South Wales Senior Australian of the Year, and he received the Australia Council's

Red Ochre Award in 2004. In the same year, he was awarded the Officer of the Order of Australia for his service to the entertainment industry as a singer, recording artist and songwriter, and to the community through reconciliation, and as an ambassador for Indigenous culture. Also in 2004 Jimmy Little was named a Living National Treasure. In 2005 the University of Sydney awarded him an honorary doctorate in music, along with composer Peter Sculthorpe, for their joint contribution to reconciliation between Indigenous and non-Indigenous Australians. He received further honorary doctorates from the Queensland University of Technology (2004) for his contribution to the Australian music industry and to Aboriginal education over forty-five years, and from the Australian Catholic University (2007).

As Jimmy's manager, Buzz Bidstrup got to know both Jimmy and Marj well. He spoke of Jimmy as a wise Uncle who had seen a lot but chose not to speak about certain things. Jimmy didn't swear, drink or smoke, and the band quickly tempered their behaviour around him. Bidstrup never signed a contract with Jimmy, but they worked together until Jimmy retired in 2011. The more Jimmy's career surged, the more people in the business wanted a piece of him. At many events, Jimmy was mobbed because everyone wanted to talk to him and take a 'selfie'. Politicians of both the left and right sides of government wanted to know him, as well as religious groups and charities.

However, when Jimmy and Marj's health began to deteriorate, there were extra challenges and responsibilities for Bidstrup. With Marj's ongoing health problems with diabetes and asthma, and then Jimmy being diagnosed with kidney failure in 2002, the relationship between Buzz and the Littles became more than a manager/client relationship. Marj and Jimmy would welcome Buzz's wife Kay and their son Maxwell into their lives as 'extended family', even though they were unrelated. When Jimmy came out of his first haemodialysis sessions with his voice sounding squeaky and hoarse, he declared that he would undertake peritoneal dialysis from then on, because it would not affect his voice and he would be able to keep on singing.

Although his workload was by then considerably reduced, Jimmy still travelled extensively across northern Australia to Aboriginal communities. He spent some time in Alice Springs and Darwin, where the state of Indigenous renal services was being hotly debated. To make a point, Jimmy did an ABC TV interview with Malarndirri McCarthy, who was a journalist at the time, but is now a senator for the Australian Labor Party in the upper house. In the interview, Jimmy showed himself undertaking dialysis, to promote the service to Aboriginal communities. Always prepared to put the hardships of others before his own, there was some irony in his message to other Indigenous people on dialysis in these remote areas, because he himself was not complying strictly with his own dialysis sessions.

Jimmy continued to work harder and harder, travelling with his dialysis equipment, while back home their house was being transformed so that Jimmy and Marj could enjoy a few more creature comforts, such as a new kitchen and bathroom. A studio and workroom were also built in his back garden, as everyone had expected that Jimmy might be headed towards retirement. However, this did not happen, because the longer he continued his visits to remote communities and rural towns, the greater the financial and social demands that were being placed on him. In these places, he was a magnet for Aboriginal people, many of whom had met him during the fifty years he had been touring.

As Jimmy's health continued to deteriorate, he went on a waiting list for a kidney transplant. Two and a half years later, in 2004, Jimmy got the call from Sydney's Royal Prince Alfred Hospital to say that one had become available. He was in Western Australia at the time, performing with James Blundell at the inaugural Days of Summer Concert in Denmark, and as far away from Sydney as you could possibly be. After frantic calls and late-night driving, he boarded a Flying Doctor Service flight from Albany to Perth, and then a commercial flight to Sydney, arriving just in time for the operation. Even as he was recuperating, he was talking about staying in the public eye. He had no intentions of retiring yet. He also talked about dedicating his time to spreading the message of hope to other kidney patients and teaching children about nutrition.

Earlier, on one of his rural and remote tours, Jimmy had met filmmaker Don Palmer, whose wife had also been a dialysis patient. Don suggested making a series of short films about dialysis and also doing a variety show for NITV, with Jimmy as the host. At around the same time, Jimmy was asked to be an ambassador for the Fred Hollows Foundation, and they began talking to Jimmy about promoting kidney health. Kidney Health Australia also wanted Jimmy to be a spokesperson and, with Jimmy's agreement, Bidstrup negotiated the terms.

Out of Jimmy's involvement with Fred Hollows Foundation came the Jimmy Little Foundation (JLF), which was formed to seek donations and then pass the funds on to other charities that would do the work on the ground. This was how an arrangement put in place with the Purple House worked. The Purple House is the informal name for the Western Desert Nganampa Walytja Palyantjaku Tjutaku Aboriginal Corporation, an Indigenous owned and run health service based in Alice Springs. When the JLF was granted money, it gave some to the Purple House, which at the time was working towards setting up a mobile renal truck. The Purple Truck, as it became known, is a self-contained dialysis unit on wheels, with two dialysis chairs, that continues to travel extensively throughout remote communities.

While the intention for the JLF had been to create programs and promote good health in Aboriginal communities, with Jimmy spreading the message that there was 'life after dialysis', as a charity the JLF had limited capabilities. However, it did manage to find extra funding for a Return to Country program, which gave patients and carers a chance to make short visits home to their remote communities between dialysis sessions. The Return to Country program was able to assist more than one hundred people, including carers and families from more than thirty remote communities in Central Australia, enabling them to return home regularly and attend important ceremonies like the Garma Festival in Yolngu Country.

As the profile of the JLF grew, so did the demand for dealing with the problem of kidney disease in these communities. In 2007 the Fred Hollows Foundation agreed to seed-fund the Uncle Jimmy's Thumbs Up! program. This nutrition program has since been funded by donations from private, corporate and philanthropic organisations and through federal, state and territory government grants. Its purpose is to educate young people in eating healthily to avoid contracting diabetes or experiencing kidney failure. Thumbs Up! has been promoting its message in a variety of ways, including music videos and health education programs, and Jimmy was involved in this until his death in 2012.

It is difficult to say how much impact the JLF and Thumbs Up! initiatives have had on Aboriginal communities across the country, but both of them have continued since Jimmy's death and do not look like closing down any time soon. The JLF, with his daughter Frances as managing director, still operates as a charity that offers scholarships and emergency funding to other charities or services in need of financial assistance. Thumbs Up! is managed by Buzz Bidstrup and continues to run its nutrition programs for school children in cities and remote regions. It is through these programs that Jimmy Little's legacy continues.

Even after receiving his kidney transplant, the extensive travel, the long days and perhaps the demands for his attention took a toll on Jimmy's life. Although his new kidney was supposed to make it easier for Jimmy, his general health was deteriorating; he needed to adjust to new medications for the kidney, and he still kept long hours. He would have kept on going if it had not been for the concerns his wife Marj had for her husband's wellbeing.

There had also been increasing problems with Marj's health and she needed him to be with her and not with the public quite so much. She had been going in and out of hospital for years with her ongoing diabetes and asthma, and now she needed his company. The plans Jimmy had to run a recording studio in his backyard to encourage and record young Aboriginal singers and musicians were just too impractical to achieve. Jimmy and Marj were reaching a point where they needed a home that would be more conducive to both their health needs and their means. It was also important that they had a home for themselves; as things stood, they were no longer in a position to be able to provide a home for the extended family members on Marj's side who lived with them. So they sold their house in Lilyfield, where they had lived for thirty years and moved to Dubbo in regional New South Wales.

Jimmy was awarded his first Golden Guitar at the Tamworth Country Music Festival prior to making the move to Dubbo, so Jimmy and Marj travelled there with their daughter Frances to receive it. Unfortunately, this trip was to take a serious toll on Marj's health. Just hours after they arrived in Tamworth, she was taken by ambulance to Tamworth Hospital, at around four in the morning. Jimmy stayed by her side the whole time until he needed to make himself available for the stream of radio interviews – and attend the awards taking place just hours later. Instead of this being a happy occasion, it turned out to be a day of conflicting emotions and sadness.

Following the Tamworth trip it became clear that it was time for Jimmy to retire from the music industry. As best he could, though, he continued to devote his time to the JLF and Thumbs Up!, even though his mind was often elsewhere.

Once they had moved to Dubbo, they found that Marj needed full-time nursing care, which only trained health workers were able to provide. Jimmy made the heartbreaking decision that she needed to be placed in care while he set up their new home. She stayed in the Dubbo Homestead Aged Care, which was part of the Dubbo Base Hospital, but before he was able to bring her home, Marj picked up an infection that set off her asthma. This then developed into pneumonia – and once again she was hospitalised. Within a matter of days, she passed away, at the age of seventy-four, on 25 July 2011.

Jimmy and Marj had been married for fifty-four years. They travelled together and came through huge changes with each other. During the times when Marj had become mostly bedridden or housebound due to her asthma and diabetes, Jimmy had worked a lot less, staying by her side as her carer and temporarily relying on the carer's pension. At that time, Jimmy reflected lovingly on their life together.

Memories are a wonderful thing to have, and the memories I have of Marj are so many, so varied, so deep, so rich and wonderful. She told me all about her dreams as a young lady. Then she put aside her dreams to fulfil my dreams. I speak a lot about my partner and my soul mate and my dear love and my best friend, she is just an ideal partner in my situation and the great love of my life, Marji.

Jimmy and Marj did as much as they could together and everyone who knew them was deeply touched by their love for one another. After Marj's death, Jimmy spent his days on his back porch, reminiscing about her and the life they had made together with Frances and James and their extended families.

Jimmy was never the same after his wife's death, although his gentleness and concern for others continued to shine through. Sadly, he could no longer sing, due to the medication and the stress on his vocal chords. His last performance was an impromptu one with an old friend and contemporary from the 1960s, Leo de Kroo. They sang a version of 'Royal Telephone' at the Seniors' Expo at Dubbo Showground. This would be his final public performance.

In the months following Marj's death, Jimmy spent a lot of time thinking through his various beliefs about his Lord, and his spiritual beliefs. He discussed his thoughts about reincarnation with his daughter and expressed his belief that he might return in some other form or as some other force. Each day, he spent several hours resting and meditating in his backyard. When Frances asked him if there was anything he might like to explore, he replied that he did not want to do anything without Marj anymore. So Frances decided it was time to take him on a journey back to Yorta Yorta Country – to Cummeragunja, where he was born, and then to the South Coast of New South Wales, to Yuin-Monaro Country, where he grew up. Together, they visited his school in Terara, as well as the graves of his mother and father. He often spoke on the phone to grandson James, who was now living and working in Melbourne, but asked Frances to monitor his phone because he did not want to speak to people who might pressure him to get back on the stage.

This was not an entirely unhappy time, but a time of reflection. When asked about his sadness, Jimmy's reply was that although his heart had been broken with the loss of his darling wife and teenage sweetheart, Marjorie Rose, he had managed to pull through the agony and find another light shining ahead of him in his remaining days.

He looked forward to fulfilling his plans for improving the lives of Aboriginal people through his foundations. He told his daughter that he was very happy with all that he had achieved and accomplished in his life and was especially happy to be comforted by his beautiful home, where he spent many hours in his garden, taking in all the natural wonders of the world and his peaceful surroundings. He was very proud of the long journey of his life and was well aware of how much love he shared with people from all walks of life, believing very strongly that the more love he gave, the more love he got back, tenfold, and the more they would then share with others.

He also told Frances that he was very fortunate in the way he found the love of his life at such an early age and how they had achieved so much together, even though they had come from such hard times and unfairness in the world. He was particularly proud of the achievements and talents of his daughter and grandson, and knew that whatever might happen to him, both of them would be strong enough (and smart enough) to take care of themselves, because they had both been instilled with all the love that he and Marj could give. He said that it was important to let people know that he had been just as grateful for the old friends and family members in his early life as he was for the new friends he had made much later in life. He felt that he loved them all equally, which was no small feat. There was no malice in his heart, no bitterness – only an enduring belief that you could spread words of love and hope through music. He hoped that his mother and father would be able to look down on him and be proud of what he had achieved. A few days after this conversation, on 2 April 2012, Jimmy died peacefully in his sleep.

The first calls put out were to his grandson James and his drummer Doug Peters. The next one was made to his former manager Buzz, who contacted the media on behalf of the family, and condolences came from everywhere, including a comment from one of his country music colleagues, Kasey Chambers, who said, 'People are not just saying nice things about him now that he's gone. People were constantly saying nice things about him while he was here'. At the Ti Tree School in the centre of the Northern Territory, the kids, along with Seraphina Presley-Haines, Seini Taumoepeau and Mal Webb, wrote a song about him, and called it 'Kumanjay Little'. Kumanjay is the name given to Aboriginal people who have died, because it is disrespectful to use the name of a person after their death. The song describes the Ti Tree kids' appreciation of all that he meant to them.

> *This is a dedication to Kumanjay Little.*
> *He was an inspiration and a generous man.*
> *He was very famous for more than fifty years.*
> *We wonder what his last words were in the last song that he sang.*
> *He had a heart for everyone who showed us how to live well.*
> *Forever smiling through his songs.*
> *Well-loved across the nation with so much to tell.*
> *Through his foundation our Uncle taught us well.*
> *Drink water, exercising and eat a balanced diet.*
> *Let's thank that Yorta Yorta Man, so gentle and quiet.*
> *Now he's watching down on us.*
> *Such a kind and respected man, forever smiling through his songs.*
> *He had a heart for everyone who showed us how to live well.*

A funeral service was held for Jimmy Little in the church where he married Marj – St Peters Church of England – and he was buried with his wife in Walgett cemetery. People travelled from far and wide for the service in this small town in a remote region of New South Wales. Some came from Yorta Yorta Country, bringing sacred sands from the Cummeragunja sandhills to throw on his coffin as it was lowered. The dancers of young Yuin-Monaro men sang loudly, telling the crowd that their voices were there to lift Jimmy's spirits to the skies where his mother and father waited for him. It was appropriate that they knew the best way to reach the spirit world was to use their voices and sing loudly. When it came time, the words from his poem 'Reincarnation' were engraved on his headstone. Today Jimmy and his beloved wife Marj are buried together in Walgett, in the Peters family section of the cemetery.

Many more people wanted to show their respects for Jimmy Little, so a memorial service was held for him on 5 May 2012. Rhoda Roberts and Buzz Bidstrup put it to the then premier of New South Wales, Barry O'Farrell, that a state service should be given in Jimmy's honour. It was agreed that it would be most appropriate for the service to be held at the Sydney Opera House rather than a church – and that the Australian and Aboriginal flags should fly high on the top of the Sydney Harbour Bridge. A concert was organised for the night of the service so that fellow singers and musicians, and people from the broader Sydney community, could attend. The performance was filmed and those artists who performed paid their respects backstage, which was captured on film, and their words are included here.

*

Jimmy Little, 2005.

Deborah Cheetham (Jimmy's niece): The first performance of *Pecan Summer* was in Mooroopna; it was about the Cummeragunja Walk-off, in which Jimmy was a babe in arms being carried by his parents. I don't like being late for a performance, but the day we performed in Mooroopna, we had to start late because there was a line-up of people waiting outside to meet Jimmy, so the show was held up until he was ready to be seated.

James Henry (Jimmy's grandson): It was special to know that he was so universally loved, among Black and White. I am very honoured to have his blood run through my veins and share his name, and have all the memories of growing up with him.

Kevin Bennett: My greatest memory of him was I did a concert with him in Tamworth. He was a little frail at the time, and he sat by the stage as I did my song. I was really nervous and thought I'd better pull out my best song. And when I walked off stage he stood up and grabbed my face with both his hands and said, 'You must keep singing that song.' It made my night. And then he signed my guitar, and he wrote, 'You are a poet with the love within, keep up the message. I hear you loud and clear.'

Judy Stone: Jimmy had the most beautiful voice and sometimes he'd come over to my grandmother's house and we'd rehearse. Well, my grandmother loved him. But then, two weeks later, a rock and roll band came over, and after they left, my grandmother said, 'You can bring Jimmy over anytime, but not that rock and roll band.'

Adam James: Pre-1967 during the White Australia policy, for Jimmy Little to come out on television and tell people that 'I don't come to you as a singer, but I come to you as a proud member of the Aboriginal race,' that was a big thing, a very courageous thing to do, especially since we weren't even considered in the census or as citizens really. He represents hope and tells us that Aboriginal people can give it a go and that we are so much more than what we are stereotyped as. And it's sad, because it cuts raw and deep with me. And I am so proud to take his name out to communities and represent his foundation.

Warren H. Williams: I remember when I did my album *Country Friends and Me*. It was a duet album, and we did 'Baby Blue', and I was incredibly proud. He came to me and asked me, 'Well, you tell me what to do,' and I thought he was like a father to me, and I'd already lost my father, but when he died, it was like I lost a father twice. A phrase he told me was: 'Don't mistake my gentleness for weakness.'

Don Walker: When I was a teenager and I used to play in all the club bands, all the guys back then idolised him, not just as a singer, but as a pretty good guitar player. His skills cut across the foundations of all versatility. You hear people and they say, 'Oh yeah, she can sing country, or he can sing pop or gospel,' but with Jimmy you just have to say, 'He can sing [anything].'

Bunna Lawrie: When I told him that my mother passed and I wrote a song for her called 'Mother', he said, 'Okay, son, let's go do it.'

Christine Anu: Jimmy was a trailblazer in the time when people only supported Aboriginal sports people. So he shined the torch for us Indigenous singers and opened up doors for us. He was a crooner, a country singer and a great storyteller.

Brendan Gallagher: Performing here tonight with Blackfellas and Whitefellas, whatever, he can bring us together. He was the embodiment of all us musicians and singers, saying, 'Come on, let's all get together and have a great time.' He was a musician's musician.

The time I started working on this album with Jimmy, Hansonism was on the rise, and I thought it would be a good time for some young Whitefella to do something with an older, wiser Blackfella. And Jimmy had such goodwill in the public and I think that's what got it over, plus he was awesomely talented.

Jeff McMullen: Jimmy always believed, from the time he was young, that he could take his guitar and just charm us. That he would win his way into your heart and open you up. When he shared that, it could be in the Sydney Opera House, or a little country town, or sitting out in the bush. The magic of those nights, out under the stars – he would come out and sing and the magic was there, letting us know that this was our cathedral. It was his heart, it wasn't a small world view, it was something he loved, and he wanted to share it.

Buzz Bidstrup: You could drive in a car with Jimmy for four hours and say nothing, and then other times we'd talk all the way, and it didn't matter, because it was the same, it was a connectedness, and you don't get that with other people unless you are talking all the time. He had a beautiful sense of humour and a wonderful disposition, and a little twinkle in his eye when he was about to say something profound. He is never going to leave me. He is always there.

Paul Kelly: Jimmy is a gentleman of the old school. I love the way he sings; he's done a couple of my songs; I've always admired him. I know a lot of people look up to him – and for a lot of the Indigenous artists, he's an Uncle to them – and he's been making music for a long time, about fifty years. You've got to tip your hat to that, because it's a pretty hard business to survive in, and he did it with grace to the end.

Shellie Morris: I would describe him as the most gentle, generous and kindest man I've met. He was full of love for everybody, full of compassion and empathy. And he was amazing at listening. And he would wait before he spoke, because he would've thought about what he had to say, and it was precious. He did a lot of amazing things for people and the world.

Casey Donovan: He wasn't just a singer; he was a man who brought people together.

Dan Sultan: He was very inspirational to me as a young man, as a singer, deadly, shit-hot musician singer, and, you know, he always had really great hair and suits, so I always looked up to him. So when I had the chance to meet him, get to know him, and, humbled to say, to become his friend. You know, he's not just once in a lifetime, he is once ever.

Neil Murray: He was a true gentleman, and had a lot of innate dignity, and one can imagine he must have had a really hard life, when you think about the time that his life spanned. He must have suffered a lot of knockbacks, but he was the sort of person that didn't let that worry him. He had a higher vision. To me, he was always buoyant, and always positive, and I can't imagine him ever saying a bad word about anyone. A true, kind man. And as far as a singer, he was world class. He had such charm in his voice, you couldn't help but be seduced by him.

Thankfully, Jimmy Little's legacy lives on through the JLF and Thumbs Up!, and many people remember him still. Since his death, his memory was honoured by Terara Public School, which planted an oak tree on its grounds, and a street was named after him in the suburb of Moncrieff in the Australian Capital Territory. And the community centre next door to where he lived in Lilyfield for thirty years, run by the Inner West council, was named The Jimmy Little Community Centre. In the township of Walgett, the local shire council have put forward an annual Jimmy Little Memorial Fund so that up-and-coming artists may apply. They also invested in a mural painted on one of the 315 square metre water towers, which has since become a part of the Australian silo trail. The image was based on a photograph taken by John Elliott and portrays Jimmy holding his guitar. The artwork was painted by artists Frank Wright (a Gamilaroi Dhunghutti man) and Jenny McCracken, who created a reflective image of Marj in both of Jimmy's eyes. Viewers can spot this if they look closely enough at the artwork.

As the words of his poem at the beginning of this chapter say, Jimmy thought he could be a torch or a key in the lives of people who suffered. Hopefully he achieved this while he was on this Earth, but whatever one may think, his voice, his message and his love are still with us in one way or another.

Notes

The author has made every effort to provide accurate internet addresses at the time of publication, however some websites are no longer accessible. Archive versions of websites have been provided where available.

1 The verses at the beginning of each chapter are either songs that Jimmy Little wrote or poems he wrote with the potential of becoming songs.

2 All paragraphs appearing as sans serif blocks of text are Jimmy's own words, as recorded in an extensive interview that the author conducted with her father: Jimmy Little, interviewed by Frances Peters-Little, Canberra, 2003.

3 Robin Ryan, 'And we marched to the tune of the Gumleaf Band but to whose tune did we march?' in Denis Crowdy, *Popular Music: Commemoration, Commodification and Communication: Proceedings of the 2004 IASPM Australia New Zealand Conference, held in conjunction with the Symposium of the International Musicological Society*, 11–16 July 2004, p. 32.

4 Personal communication from AIATSIS film archivist Michael Leigh, 7 February 1994, in Ryan, 'And we marched to the tune of the Gumleaf Band ...'

5 Alick Jackomos, 'Gumleaf Bands', *Identity*, vol. 1 no. 1, July 1971, in Ryan, 'And we marched to the tune of the Gumleaf Band ...', p. 32.

6 Merle Jackomos in Alick Jackomos and Derek Fowell (eds), *Living Aboriginal History of Victoria: Stories in the Oral Tradition*, Cambridge University Press, Melbourne, 1991, p. 170.

7 Ryan, 'And we marched to the tune of the Gumleaf Band ...', pp. 25–8.

8 Victoria Museum, *Bunjilaka newsletter*, 2005, p. 13. It was first cited at http://museumsvictoria.com.au/Bunjilaka, however the link no longer includes an archive of previous newsletters.

9   *Pix* also published a story about Edwin Atkinson's choir in 1941, in *Pix* magazine, 15 November 1941, p. 37. Established in 1938 and read by people of all 'walks of life', *Pix* was one of Australia's most popular magazines during the 1950s, 1960s and 1970s.

10 Laurel Robinson of the Sapphires, an all-girl group that toured from Victoria to Vietnam (Laurel and her niece Lois Peeler being the ones to tour Vietnam), spoke briefly about Cummeragunja's musical history in an interview with the *Sydney Morning Herald*, in an article, 'Questions for Laurel Robinson', on 16 January 2005.

11 Illustration cited in Bain Attwood and Andrew Markus, *Thinking Black*, Aboriginal Studies Press, Canberra, 2004, p. 72.

12 Jimmy Little, interviewed by Frances Peters-Little, Canberra, 2003.

13 Yorta Yorta Nation Aboriginal Corporation, Yorta Yorta Country, https://yynac.com.au/yorta-yorta-country/.

14 Stewart Taylor and Bella Kennedy, Murray Lower Darling Rivers, Indigenous Nations, Wamba Wamba, https://www.mldrin.org.au/membership/.

15 Barapa Barapa Land and Water, Barapa Barapa Country, History, https://barapa.org.au/barapa-barapa/.

16 Richard Broome, *Aboriginal Victorians: A history since 1800*, Allen and Unwin, Sydney, 2005, p. 258.

17 Broome, *Aboriginal Victorians*, p. 258.

18 Janet McGee's death certificate. B. 1873 Swan Hill D. 1939 Echuca. Death certificate Victoria 18588.

19 Aboriginal Welfare Board Records, Kendall Database, 21/09/1899, frame number 341, reel no. 2789, p. 5.

20 Anna Morgan, 'Under the Black Flag', *Labor Call*, 20 September 1934, cited in Bain Attwood and Andrew Markus, *Thinking Black: William Cooper and the Australian Aborigines' League*, Aboriginal Studies Press, Canberra, 2004, p. 42. Morgan writes, 'Those who protested against this injustice were classed as agitators, an expulsion order was made out against them, and it was served by the local police'.

21 Attwood and Markus, *Thinking Black*, p. 59.

22 Aboriginal Welfare Board Records, 1897.

23 Bounded by the Edward River and Colligen and Tumudgeri Creeks, Moonacullah Mission took its name from the word 'Moonacullah', meaning 'place of many waters'.

24 Moonacullah, 24 March 1915 correspondence to the Aboriginal Protection Board of Education.
25 Moonacullah, 16 August 1915 correspondence to the Aboriginal Protection Board of Education.
26 George McGee's death certificate. B. 1858 D. 1903 Wanganella NSW. Death certificate NSW 13576/1903.
27 Ernest McGee and Janet Ingram, Marriage 1901, New South Wales Births, Deaths and Marriages Registration Act 1995, Registration Number 1901/004278.
28 Barham is the sister town to Koondrook, which is on the Victorian side of the Murray, and Barham in New South Wales, but both towns are on the Murray River.
29 Attwood and Markus, *Thinking Black*, p. 21.
30 Attwood and Markus, *Thinking Black*, p. 21.
31 Heather Goodall, 'A history of Aboriginal communities in New South Wales, 1909–1939', unpublished PhD Thesis, University of Sydney, NSW, 1982, p. 390.
32 Goodall, 'A history of Aboriginal communities in New South Wales', p. 390.
33 Goodall, 'A history of Aboriginal communities in New South Wales', p. 392.
34 Goodall, 'A history of Aboriginal communities in New South Wales', p. 392.
35 Attwood and Markus, *Thinking Black*. The authors write, 'William Cooper was the founder and leader of the Australian Aborigines' League, the most important of the first crop of Aboriginal political organisations formed in Australia. In the 1920s and 1930s, other bodies were founded in settled Australia, principally the Australian Aboriginal Progressive Association, the Native Union and the Aborigines Progressive Association. However, these were short-lived and had a narrower focus than Cooper's League.'
36 Goodall, 'A history of Aboriginal communities in New South Wales', p. 393.
37 'Cummeragunja', *Mission Voices*. This site has since been removed, an archived version of the site is available at: https://web.archive.org/web/20040922061047/http://www.abc.net.au/missionvoices/cummeragunja/voices_of_cummerangunja/uncle_sandy_atkinson/uncle_sandy_talks_of_nanny_nora/default.htm.

38 'At Cummeroogunya Reserve in the last 22 months the death-toll was six adults, four children, and fifteen babies died at birth, it was alleged yesterday', 'Aboriginal Charges Cruelty' in *Daily Telegraph*, 1 December 1938, cited in Attwood and Markus, *Thinking Black*, p. 108.

39 Jimmy Little, interviewed by Frances Peters-Little, Canberra, 2003.

40 Goodall, 'A history of Aboriginal communities in New South Wales', p. 400.

41 Goodall, 'A history of Aboriginal communities in New South Wales', p. 406.

42 Goodall, 'A history of Aboriginal communities in New South Wales', p. 407.

43 Broome, *Aboriginal Victorians*, p. 264.

44 'Tatura Internment Group was the first purpose-built internment camp for World War II. It consisted of four camps – two at Tatura and two at Rushworth. Camps No. 1 and No. 2 at Tatura were located less than a kilometre from each other. Camps No. 3 and No. 4 were located at Rushworth, a couple of kilometres from Tatura, and are sometimes known as Rushworth No. 3 and No. 4 camps.' Originally cited at http://www.naa.gov.au/whats-on/online/feature-exhibits/internment-camps/wwii/tatura.aspx/, however the link is no longer active.

45 The Aborigines Welfare Board was created in 1940 to replace the Aborigines Protection Board. Although it was set up under the *Aborigines Protection (Amendment) Act 1940* with the intention of modernising Aboriginal welfare, in reality it continued many of the policies towards children that were in place under the protection board. It was abolished and replaced by the Aborigines Welfare Directorate in 1969. Cited at https://www.findandconnect.gov.au/guide/nsw/NE00033.

46 Foreign is the word Jimmy used to describe his uncomfortable feelings about Koondrook.

47 Quote from a letter by William Cooper as the Secretary of the Australian Aborigines' League, to the Chairman, of the Aborigines Protection Board, New South Wales, Sydney, 28 November 1938. Cited in Attwood and Markus, *Thinking Black*, p. 107.

48 Ernest McGee death certificate, b. 1874 d. 1940 NSW Death Registration Transcription Reference No. 1940/11871.

49   Jimmy Little, interviewed by Frances Peters-Little, Canberra, 2003.

50   They may not have been officially married.

51   Dry River commences about 10 kilometres west of Cobargo, in the Great Dividing Range, and flows in a south-east direction, joining with Mumbulla Creek to form the Murrah River.

52   Jimmy Little, interviewed by Robin Hughes, *Australian Biography: Jimmy Little*, Film Australia, 1998.

53   Harold Harrison, interviewed by Stolen Generations Testimonies, cited at https://www.stolengenerationstestimonies.com/harold-harrison.html. The interview is on video, the quote begins at 1:53.

54   Umbarra is the Pacific black duck. It is the totem for the Yuin area.

55   'Gulaga Mountain is the place of ancestral origin within the mythology of the Yuin People, she is the mother of Yuin Man, and many believe the mother of all man'. Cited in Lisa Herbert, 'A momentous gathering of the Yuin Nation to heal country and spirit', *About Regional*, 30 November 2019, https://aboutregional.com.au/a-momentous-gathering-of-the-yuin-nation-to-heal-country-and-spirit/.

56   Jimmy Little, interviewed by Robin Hughes, *Australian Biography: Jimmy Little*.

57   Jimmy Little, interviewed by Robin Hughes, *Australian Biography: Jimmy Little*.

58   Ryan, 'And we marched to the tune of the Gumleaf Band ...', p. 27.

59   Janet Mathews, Language elicitation and songs from the South Coast, NSW, 1965, AIATSIS, Canberra.

60   Australian Frontier Conflicts 1788–1940s, at https://australianfrontierconflicts.com.au/.

61   'Thousands of Aboriginal children provided European settlers with essential labour in a range of different occupations in Queensland between 1842 and 1945 ... male Aboriginal children were predominantly employed as pastoral workers ... [or] employed in the pearling and beche-de-mer industry. There are also accounts of Aboriginal children working as guides and interpreters; on the goldfields; as "errand boys"; labourers; in circuses and as jockeys.' Cited in Shirleene Rose Robinson, 'Something like slavery'?: The exploitation of Aboriginal child labour in Queensland, 1842–1945, PhD Thesis, University of Queensland, 2003.

62　The laws under the *Aboriginals Protection and Restriction of the Sale of Opium Act 1897* appeared to be far more oppressive than the laws that governed New South Wales.

63　Other records my father and I discussed were the Tindale records of Wallaga Lake, which note that Jack Little was from Queensland, and his police salary records at Emu Flat in 1901, the same year his census records place him as living at Emu Flat prior to 1901. There were records from the Aboriginal Welfare Board which say Jack Little was issued a rail pass on 27 September 1900 from Goulburn railway station to the Manning Valley. The return date of his rail pass was 28 October, which incidentally was the day after Aboriginal bushranger/outlaw Jimmy Governor was captured at dawn and jailed at Wingham in the Manning Valley region. My father and I could only speculate that Jack Little was called upon to participate in the extensive search for Governor and his brother Joe, who had been mercilessly pursued by countless bloodhounds and hundreds of police and civilians and trackers from Queensland and New South Wales. John Edward Little died on 2 March 1932 at Wallaga Lake Aboriginal Station, death registry no. 2155/1932.

64　Archival taped interviews by Janet Mathews with Jimmy Little Snr., 1964.

65　Jimmy Little, interviewed by Robin Hughes, *Australian Biography: Jimmy Little*.

66　Jimmy Little, interviewed by Frances Peters-Little, Canberra, 2003.

67　Clinton Walker, *Buried Country*, Pluto Press, 2000, p. 32.

68　The Logie Award-winning singing competition *Australian Idol* made its television debut in July 2003. There have been two Aboriginal winners of *Australian Idol*, both women: Casey Donovan, who won in 2004, and Jessica Mauboy, who won in 2006.

69　Richard Lane, *The Golden Age of Australian Radio Drama, 1923–1960: A History through Biography*, MUP, 1994, p. 3.

70　Arrow, *Friday on our Minds: Popular Culture since 1945*, UNSW Press, 2009, p. 9.

71　Michelle Arrow, *Friday on our Minds*, p. 21.

72　The British record label Regal Zonophone was formed in 1932 as a merger of the Regal and Zonophone labels when the parent companies of these labels merged to become EMI. EMI Records Ltd was established in 1956 as the record manufacturing and distribution arm of EMI in the UK.

73 Founded in Sydney in 1952, Festival Records (which in 1999 amalgamated with Mushroom Records to become Festival Mushroom Records) became a successful Australian recording and publishing company that operated until 2005.

74 Jimmy Little, interviewed by Frances Peters-Little, Canberra, 2003.

75 'Danny Boy' was written by F. Weatherly and 'Lucky Old Sun' was written by H. Gillespie and B. Smith. 'El Paso' was written by M. Robbins and 'The Last Rose of Summer' was composed by F. Von Flotow.

76 Auriel Andrew OAM was born in Darwin in 1947 and grew up in Alice Springs. At the age of twenty-one she headed to Adelaide to pursue a career in music, moving to Sydney at Jimmy's encouragement, and continuing her music career until her death at age sixty-nine.

77 Col moved from his hometown of Brewarrina to Sydney in 1962 to further his musical career. He was a member of the country band the Opals, which at times was the house band for Jimmy when he performed as part of the All Coloured Revue. Cited at https://www.floreena.com/australian-pioneers-of-country-music.html.

78 Interview with Richard Guilliatt, 'The two of us', *Good Weekend, The Sydney Morning Herald*, 17 July 1999.

79 'Features of the administration of the board included the implementation of the assimilation policy and, from the early 1950s, the movement of Aboriginal people to where they could be prepared for absorption into the general community and persuaded to share the life in the towns with Whites.' Cited in Anita Heiss, 'Government policy in relation to Aboriginal people', *Barani: Sydney's Aboriginal History, City of Sydney*, https://www.sydneybarani.com.au/sites/government-policy-in-relation-to-aboriginal-people/.

80 Marj became the eldest after her older brother, Fredrick Peters, died from polio at Balmain Hospital in 1953.

81 Interview with Marjorie Little, Lilyfield, 2009.

82 Interview with Jane Hickey, *Australian Woman's Weekly*, 13 April 1966.

83 See Heidi Norman, 'A modern day Corroboree: towards a history of the New South Wales Aboriginal Rugby League Knockout', *Aboriginal History*, vol. 30, 2006, pp. 169–186.

84 Malcolm D. Prentis, *A Concise Companion of Aboriginal History*, Rosenberg Publishing, 2008, p. 179.

85 Melinda Hinkson and Alana Harris, *Aboriginal Sydney*, Aboriginal Studies Press, Canberra, 2001, p. 107.

86 The *All Coloured Show* was an all-Indigenous revue spearheaded by Jimmy and his manager Ted Quigg.

87 *Dawn* and *New Dawn* were Australian monthly magazines published from January 1952 until July 1975 by the New South Wales Aboriginal Welfare Board, with Aboriginal people their intended readership.

88 It was common knowledge to the family that Lillian could not have written such a letter.

89 'Miss Peters Comes to Town', letter, *Dawn* magazine, vol. 3 issue 11, p. 21.

90 Doreen Peters, interviewed by Frances Peters-Little, University of Sydney, Sydney, 1991.

91 A politician and inspector of Aborigines, Robert Thomas Donaldson (1851–1936) would design and oversee the implementation of three Aborigines Protection Acts which gave more and more control to the Aborigines Protection Board. He was notorious in Aboriginal communities for his racist views and treatment of Aboriginal children.

92 Walgett sits at the junction of the Barwon and Namoi rivers. These rivers are the natural boundaries for two traditional language groups, Gamilaraay and Yuwaalaraay, which share the shire. There is a mission and a reserve on the outskirts of Walgett, with the mission, Gingie, located on the Barwon River.

93 The Namoi Reserve, on the north side of the Walgett levee bank on the Namoi River, is about three kilometres from Gingie Mission.

94 Charles Benedict Davenport, 'Notes on physical anthropology of Australian Aborigines and black-white hybrids', *American Journal of Physical Anthropology*, vol. 8, no. 1, 1925, pp. 73–94.

95 *Dawn* magazine, 1959, vol. 8, issue 3, p. 14.

96 Nathan Lum, 'Popular culture – Australian entertainment in the 1960's', 19 November 2013, https://prezi.com/cdjbaiccm_f_/popular-culture-australian-entertainment-in-the-1960s/.

97 B. B. Schweiger & D. G. Matthews (eds), *Religion in the American South: Protestants and Others in History and Culture*, p. 128.

98 'Royal Telephone', lyrics, see http://www.hymntime.com/tch/htm/r/o/y/a/royaltel.htm.

99 Data from Religious Affiliation Over Time - 1966, 1991, 2016, ABS Census of Population and Housing.

100 Tommy Tycho, interviewed by Sean Kennedy in *Jimmy Little's Gentle Journey*, ABC TV, 2003. This 55-minute video was written and directed by Sydney-based filmmaker Sean Kennedy and released by Indigo Films and Warner Vision Australia.

101 Jimmy's scrapbook.

102 'First Awards Go To Aussies', *Billboard* magazine, 4 April, 1964, p. 4.

103 Tracey Moffatt, quoted in Scott Murray, 'Tracey Moffatt: Night cries: a rural tragedy', *Cinema Papers*, no. 79, May 1990, p. 22.

104 Judy Stone was a regular on Brian Henderson's *Bandstand* throughout the 1960s. She had numerous top 20 singles. Cited at https://wikimili.com/en/Judy_Stone.

105 At the peak of his sixty-year music career, Lee had numerous top 100 singles. Cited at https://www.australialive.org.au/artists/lonnie-lee/.

106 Over his sixty-year music career, Col Joye had numerous successes on the Australian rock and roll charts, and was the first Australian rock and roll artist to have a number one across the country; he didn't restrict himself to one genre, he has also recorded country music and other cross-over styles, as well as being an entrepreneur within the music scene. Cited at https://northsideradio.com.au/shows/rons-golden-oldies/featured-artist-this-week-col-joye/.

107 Jimmy Little, interviewed by Sean Kennedy in *Jimmy Little's Gentle Journey*.

108 Jimmy Little, interviewed by Robin Hughes, *Australian Biography: Jimmy Little*.

109 Jeanie Bell, 'In my mind when you hear someone using the work "blacks", I, as an Aboriginal person, associate it with colonial language generally spoken in harsh tones with a sense of utter dismissal and bordering on hatred or strong resentment, such as "the dirty blacks" or "drunken or lazy blacks", etc. All of which I find extremely offensive and know many others who would also.' Quoted in 'Can the media call indigenous Australians "blacks"?, *Crikey*, 2 Feb 2012, https://www.crikey.com.au/2012/02/02/can-indigenous-australians-be-called-blacks/.

110 The Gamilaraay, or Kamilaroi, are one of the four largest Australian First Nations language groups, whose Country extends from New South Wales into southern Queensland.

111 Max Ellis, 'A Tribute to Jimmy Little', *History of Country Music in Australia*, https://www.historyofcountrymusic.com.au/tributetojimmy.html.

112 'Australian Country Music News', *Country Music Bulletin*, https://www.countrymusicbulletin.com.au/newsarchive_Jan11.html.

113 H. Reynolds, *Aborigines and Settlers: The Australian Experience 1788–1939*, Cassell Australia, Sydney, 1972, p. 175.

114 Betty Little, Jimmy's sister, even stated in an interview on ABC TV that she would have liked Jimmy to be more political and that he was not active enough.

115 Excerpt from *Monday Conference (1971–1979)*, a 60-minute current affairs program on ABC TV, cited in Kennedy, *Jimmy Little's Gentle Journey*.

116 Marj Little, interviewed by Sean Kennedy in *Jimmy Little's Gentle Journey*.

117 Cyril Green, interviewed over the phone by Frances Peters-Little, Armidale, 2021.

118 Frances Peters-Little, interviewed by Sean Kennedy in *Jimmy Little's Gentle Journey*.

119 'Running Commentary', Daphne Caruana Galizia's Notebook, at https://daphnecaruanagalizia.com/2013/08/a-man-of-black-skin-with-a-pure-white-heart/.

120 *Australian Dictionary of Biography*, http://adb.anu.edu.au/biography/jackey-jackey-2264.

121 Urban slang, British Dictionary, https://www.dictionary.com/browse/coconut.

122 Alan T. Duncan, 'Blair, Harold (1924–1976)', *Australian Dictionary of Biography*, http://adb.anu.edu.au/biography/blair-harold-9520.

123 Bob McLeod, quoted in Kennedy, *Jimmy Little's Gentle Journey*.

124 'The Coloured Lad' was written by Jimmy's father, Kunkus Little, and expresses his frustrations with racism and the way Aboriginal people were being treated, particularly in regards to employment opportunities. Jimmy first recorded the song in 1959.

125 Heather Goodall, *Invasion to Embassy: Land in Aboriginal Politics in New South Wales, 1770–1972*, Sydney University Press, 2008, p. 148.

126 I know of these people because they either visited our home or they were often spoken about in our home.
127 Jimmy Little, interviewed by Frances Peters-Little, Canberra, 2003.
128 Kennedy, *Jimmy Little's Gentle Journey*.
129 Eileen Perkins, interviewed over the phone by Frances Peters-Little, Sydney, 2020.
130 Kennedy, *Jimmy Little's Gentle Journey*.
131 Kennedy, *Jimmy Little's Gentle Journey*.
132 Kennedy, *Jimmy Little's Gentle Journey*.
133 Zoe Pollock, 'Foundation for Aboriginal Affairs', *Dictionary of Sydney*, State Library of New South Wales, 2008, https://dictionaryofsydney.org/entry/foundation_for_aboriginal_affairs.
134 *Paul Coe*, Tent Embassy film by Frances Peters-Little, 1992.
135 Jimmy Little, interviewed by Frances Peters-Little, Canberra, 2003.
136 Jimmy Little, interviewed by Robin Hughes, *Australian Biography: Jimmy Little*, Film Australia, 1998.
137 Jimmy Little, interviewed by Robin Hughes, *Australian Biography: Jimmy Little*, Film Australia, 1998.
138 Jimmy Little, interviewed by Frances Peters-Little, Canberra, 2003.
139 Jimmy Little, interviewed by Frances Peters-Little, Canberra, 2003.
140 James Henry, interviewed by Sean Kennedy in *Jimmy Little's Gentle Journey*.
141 Production information regarding *Black River* is available at https://www.screenaustralia.gov.au/the-screen-guide/t/black-river-1993/961/.
142 Production information regarding *Somewhere in the Darkness* is available at https://www.screenaustralia.gov.au/the-screen-guide/t/somewhere-in-the-darkness-1999/13247/.
143 Jimmy Little, interviewed by Sean Kennedy in *Jimmy Little's Gentle Journey*.
144 Jimmy Little, interviewed by Frances Peters-Little, Canberra, 2003.
145 Brendan Gallagher, interviewed via email by Frances Peters-Little, Lightning Ridge, 2021.
146 Brendan Gallagher, interviewed via email by Frances Peters-Little, Lightning Ridge, 2021.

147 Marj Little, interviewed by Sean Kennedy in *Jimmy Little's Gentle Journey*.

148 Jimmy Little, interviewed by Sean Kennedy in *Jimmy Little's Gentle Journey*.

149 Brendan Gallagher, interviewed via email by Frances Peters-Little, Lightning Ridge, 2021.

150 Jimmy Little, interviewed by Sean Kennedy in *Jimmy Little's Gentle Journey*.

151 Jimmy Little, interviewed by Robin Hughes, *Australian Biography: Jimmy Little*, Film Australia, 1998.

152 Brendan Gallagher, interviewed via email by Frances Peters-Little, Lightning Ridge, 2021.

153 Brendan Gallagher, interviewed via email by Frances Peters-Little, Lightning Ridge, 2021.

154 Leah Purcell, interviewed by Sean Kennedy in *Jimmy Little's Gentle Journey*.

155 Glenn A. Baker, interviewed by Sean Kennedy in *Jimmy Little's Gentle Journey*.

156 Brendan Gallagher, interviewed via email by Frances Peters-Little, Lightning Ridge, 2021.

157 Jimmy Little, interviewed by Robin Hughes, 1998.

158 Jimmy Little, interviewed by Robin Hughes, 1998.

159 Jimmy Little, interviewed by Robin Hughes, 1998.

160 Jimmy Little, interviewed by Robin Hughes, 1998.

Appendix

Discography: Solo albums

YOU'LL NEVER WALK ALONE

1960	Festival Records	LP
You'll Never Walk Alone	Beyond The Sunset	
Trees	You Should Go First	
If I Can Help Somebody	Ol' Man River	
I Believe	Goin' My Way	
The Last Rose Of Summer	Whispering Hope	
Danny Boy	That Lucky Old Sun	
The Bells Of St Marys		

SING TO GLORY

1963	Festival Records	LP
I Am On The Battlefield	When The Saints Go Marching In	
Royal Telephone	Hornets	
Just A Closer Walk	Life's Railway To Heaven	
The Church In The Wildwood	Old Time Religion	
By And By	Each Step Of The Way	
Somebody's Knocking At Your Door	Answer The Call Of Jesus	

A TREE IN THE MEADOW

1963	Festival Records	LP
A Tree In The Meadow	Land Of The Sundown	
Walk Me By The River	Marie	
The Little Green Valley	It's Worth The Price You Pay	
Rock Island Line	Marie Elena	
Home On The Range	Smile	
Galway Bay	Please	

ROYAL TELEPHONE AND OTHER SONGS OF FAITH

1965	Festival Records	LP
His Faith In Me	Royal Telephone	
Blessed Assurance	He's Got The Whole World In His Hands	
Who Is On The Lord's Side	Stand Up For Jesus	
Crown Him With Many Crowns	Hold The Fort	
Praise My Soul The King Of Heaven	Way Of The Cross	
Silent Night	Story Of The Way Of The Cross	

ONWARD CHRISTIAN SOLDIER

1965	Festival Records	LP
Onward Christian Soldiers	I Heard The Voice Of Jesus Say	
All People That On Earth Do Dwell	Stand Up For Jesus	
He's Got The Whole World In His Hands	Lead Kindly Light	
Fight The Good Fight	Hold The Fort	
Nearer My God Thee	Holy Holy Holy	
One Road	Lifeline	

JIMMY LITTLE SINGS THE COUNTRY AND WESTERN GREATS

1965	Festival Records	LP
Lonesome Number One	I Can't Help It	
Born To Lose	I Can Mend A Broken Heart	
The Gal Who Invented Kissing	Treasures Untold	
Still	There Wasn't An Organ At Our Wedding	
I Really Don't Want To Know	Little Old You	
Take Good Care Of Her	El Paso	

ENCORES

1967	Universal Record Club	LP
Eternally	Someone's Pushing Me	
Mary Said	Too Many Parties	
Marie	Rock Island Line	
Please	Kissing Someone New	
No One Will Ever Know	Pledge Of Love	
Little By Little	Long Time To Forget	

BALLADS AND STRINGS

1967	Festival Records	LP
Moonlight And Roses	Stars Fell On Alabama	
Its Not For Me To Say	There Goes My Heart	
You Belong To My Heart	You Belong To Me	
Melody Of Love	I'm Walking Right Behind You	
As Time Goes By	In The Chapel In The Moonlight	
There Must Be A Way	Always In My Heart	

NEW SONGS FROM JIMMY

1967	Festival Records	LP
Little By Little	Walking Talking Teardrops	
The Ballad Of Sleepy Mountain	If I Didn't Love You So Much	
Too Many Times	Too Many Twisted Trails	
Pictures On My Mind	One Silver Peso	
I'll Remember You My Friend	Its No Wonder	
Don't Try To Pretend	Too Many Kisses	

COUNTRY BOY COUNTRY HITS

1968	Festival Records	LP
Oh Lonesome Me	High Noon	
Green Green Grass Of Home	Singing The Blues	
Bye Bye Love	Release Me	
Streets Of Laredo	I'm So Lonesome I Could Cry	
He'll Have To Go	Hey Good Lookin'	
I Love You Because	Kaw-Liga	

MY COUNTRY

1968	Festival Records	LP
My Country	Sometime Lovin'	
When The Rain Tumbles Down In July	Little Boy Lost	
Never Never	Velvet Waters	
Reminiscing	Click Go The Shears	
Waltzing Matilda	Boomerang	
Sun Arise	I Found A New Love	

THE COUNTRY SOUND OF JIMMY LITTLE

1969   **Festival Records**   **LP**

Oh Lonesome Me	Lonesome Number One
Green Green Grass Of Home	Born To Lose
Bye Bye Love	The Gal Who Invented Kissing
Streets Of Laredo	Still
He'll Have To Go	I Really Don't Want To Know
I Love You Because	Take Good Care Of Her

I CAN'T STOP LOVING YOU

1971   **Karussell**   **LP**

I Can't Stop Loving You	By The Time I Got To Phoenix
Gentle On My Mind	Anytime
Ring Of Fire	Love Me Tender
Six Days On The Road	Be Honest With Me
Half As Much	(Just) Like Walkin' In The Sand
One Dozen Roses	Near You

GOODBYE OLD ROLF

1971   **Universal Summit**   **LP**

Send Me The Pillow You Dream On	Hello Mary Lou
Engine Engine Number 9	Another Fool Like Me
Goodbye Old Rolf	King Of The Road
Am I That Easy To Forget	Why Oh Mummy Why
Things	A White Sports Coat
Little Imp Of Baringa	Do What You Do Do Well

WALTZING MATILDA

1972 — Horizon — LP

Waltzing Matilda	My Country
Never Never	One Silver Peso
Little Imp Of Baringa	Sun Arise
Click Go The Shears	Don't Try To Pretend
Too Many Twisted Trails	Reminiscing
Little Boy Lost	Why Oh Mummy Why

WINTERWOOD

1972 — Festival Records — LP

Back In The Race	There's A Heartache Following Me
A Simple Thing As Love	Winterwood
Ann	Husbands And Wives
Wildflower	The Gentle Of A Man
Walking On The Fighting Side Of Me	All I Ever Need Is You
It Takes Time	Marry Me

BY REQUEST

1973 — Festival Records — LP

A Tree In The Meadow	Danny Boy
Whispering Hope	I'll Take You Home Again Kathleen
A Man Called Peter	Bells Of St Marys
Little Green Valley	Galway Bay
You'll Never Walk Alone	Smile
That Lucky Old Sun	El Paso

ALL FOR LOVE

1975	Festival Records	LP
Ain't It Good To Feel This Way	Dance With Me One More Time	
Goodbye Isn't Really Good At All	You're The One	
Angel In An Apron	I Wouldn't Want To Live If You Didn't Love Me	
All For The Love Of A Girl	Turn It Over In Your Mind	
Love Is Here	Baby Blue	
All My Roads Lead Back To You	Such A Lovely Day	

AN EVENING WITH JIMMY LITTLE LIVE AT THE SYDNEY OPERA HOUSE

1978	Festival Records	LP
Introduction	Still	
I Love You More And More Everyday	Come To Me	
I Love You Because	Never Ending Song Of Love	
All Over Again/I Walk The Line	Tennessee Waltz	
Room Full Of Roses	Oh Lonesome Me	
On The Street Where You Live	Steel Guitar Rag (Instrumental)	
One Dozen Roses	There Goes My Everything	
Twelth Of Never	Baby Blue	
Mexicali Rose	Australia Downunder	
Danny Boy	Royal Telephone	
Pearly Shells	May The Force Always Be With You	
He'll Have To Go		

YORTA YORTA MAN

1995	Monitor	CD
Yorta Yorta Man	The Man From Downunder	
Stealing My Heart Away	Sacred Place	
Holding You	Too Old To Learn	
Rising When We All Fall	Ngarlareen	
A Blessing In Disguise	Used To Be A Love Song	
Kimberley Moon	Nobody Else	
There's A Shadow On The Moon Tonight	Australia Downunder	

MESSENGER

1999	Festival Records	CD
Down Below	Cattle And Cane	
Under The Milky Way	(Are You) The One That I've Been Waiting For	
The Way I Made You Feel	Blackfella Whitefella	
Randwick Bells	Alone With You	
Quasimodo's Dream	Bring Yourself Home To Me	
Into Temptation		

RESONATE

2001	Festival Mushroom	CD
Surely God Is A Lover	Now That You've Gone	
You Put A Spell On Me	Love Is Mighty Close To You	
Seven Sisters	The River Of Love	
Bury Me Deep In Love	Only You	
Resonate In Blue	I Still Believe	
This Is The Truth		

LIVE AT THE STUDIO SYDNEY OPERA HOUSE

2001 — **Warner Records** — **CD**

Under The Milky Way	Australia Downunder
Cattle And Cane	Into Temptation
Randwick Bells	Blackfella Whitefella
Alone With You	Wide Open Road
Quasimodo's Dream	It's A Long Way To The Top
Can't Help Falling In Love With You	Almost With You
Royal Telephone	Family Man
Shadow Of The Boomerang	The Way I Made You Feel

DOWN THE ROAD

2003 — **ABC Records** — **CD**

Down The Road	There Must Be A Way
I Don't Know Why I Love You But I Do	Summer Rain
Reach Out	A Reason For It All
All Your Future Days	Pearls Of Wisdom
Before You Fall	Living A Lie
Smooth Sailing	When I Dream
Give Me My Guitar	

LIFE'S WHAT YOU MAKE IT

2004 — **Festival Mushroom** — **CD**

Under The Bridge	One Line
People Get Ready	In My Room
Look Out For My Love	My Father's House
Life's What You Make It	On The Sacred Sand
One	Stand By Me
What's So Funny About Peace Love & Understanding	

Discography: Compilation albums

THE BEST OF JIMMY LITTLE

1967	Festival Records	LP
Royal Telephone	Goodbye Old Rolf	
I Can't Stop Loving You	El Paso	
Gentle On My Mind	Old Time Religion	
Six Days On The Road	Little Boy Lost	
Hello Mary Lou	By The Time I Got To Phoenix	
Stand Up For Jesus	Danny Boy	
The Bells Of St Marys		

COUNTRY SOUNDS

1974	Festival Records	LP
I Can't Stop Loving You	Oh Lonesome Me	
Gentle On My Mind	Green Green Grass Of Home	
Ring Of Fire	Bye Bye Love	
Six Days On The Road	Streets Of Laredo	
Half As Much	He'll Have To Go	
One Dozen Roses	I Love You Because	
By The Time I Get To Phoenix	High Noon	
Anytime	Singing The Blues	
Love Me Tender	Release Me	
Be Honest With Me	I'm So Lonesome I Could Cry	
Just Walking In The Rain	Hey Good Looking	
Near You	Kaw-Liga	

SINGS COUNTRY

1976	Universal Summit	LP
Oh Lonesome Me	I Can't Stop Loving You	
Green Green Grass Of Home	Gentle On My Mind	
Bye Bye Love	Ring Of Fire	
Streets Of Laredo	Six Days On The Road	
He'll Have To Go	Half As Much	
I Love You Because	One Dozen Roses	
Lonesome Number One	By The Time I Get To Phoenix	
Born To Lose	Anytime	
The Gal Who Invented Kissing	Love Me Tender	
Still	Be Honest With Me	
I Really Don't Want To Know	Just Walking In The Rain	
Take Good Care Of Her	Near You	

THE BEST OF JIMMY LITTLE

1977	Festival Records	LP
Baby Blue	Royal Telephone	
Gentle On My Mind	A Tree In The Meadow	
I Can't Stop Loving You	Galway Bay	
Danny Boy	Molly	
A Man Called Peter	Old Shep	
El Paso	Rock Island Line	
You'll Never Walk Alone	Velvet Waters	
Waltzing Matilda	Goodbye Old Rolf	

20 GOLDEN COUNTRY GREATS: JIMMY LITTLE

1979	Festival Records	LP
Baby Blue	Royal Telephone	
May The Force Always Be With You	Winterwood	
I Love You Because	I Can't Stop Loving You	
One Dozen Roses	Say It Again	
Ain't It Good	He'll Have To Go	
Love Me Tender	There's A Heartache Following Me	
From Woman To Woman	A Man Called Peter	
Six Days On The Road	Near You	
Kaw-Liga	All My Roads Lead Back To You	
Travelling Minstrel Man	Ring Of Fire	

THE BEST OF JIMMY LITTLE

1992	Festival Records	LP
Baby Blue	A Tree In The Meadow	
Gentle On My Mind	Galway Bay	
I Just Can't Stop Loving You	Molly	
Danny Boy	Old Shep	
A Man Called Peter	Rock Island Line	
El Paso	Velvet Waters	
You'll Never Walk Alone	Goodbye Old Rolf	
Waltzing Matilda	Beautiful Woman	
Royal Telephone	Is This Love	

PASSAGE

2002	Warner Records	CD
Danny Boy	Baby Blue	
Little By Little	Australia Downunder	
Shadow Of The Boomerang	Dance With Me	
Kissing Someone New	Goodbye Isn't Really Good At All	
Mary Said	I Wouldn't Want To Live If You Didn't Love Me	
Little Green Valley	Mexicali Rose	
Too Many Parties & Too Many Pals	I Love You More And More Everyday	
Royal Telephone	Pearly Shells	
One Road	Beautiful Woman	
Smile	Is This Love	
Eternally	Down Below	
Christmas In The Air	Under The Milky Way	
Too Many Time	The Way I Made You Feel	
Walking Talking Teardrop	Thank You For The Dreamtime	
Wildflower	Surely God Is A Lover	
Husbands And Wives	You Put A Spell On Me	
There's A Heartache Following Me	This Is The Truth	
Anne		

THE DEFINITIVE COLLECTION

2004   **Warner Records**   **CD**

Danny Boy	Winterwood
Little By Little	Baby Blue
Shadow Of The Boomerang	Australia Downunder
Kissing Someone New	Dance With Me
Mary Said	Goodbye Isn't Really Good At All
Little Green Valley	I Wouldn't Want To Live If You Didn't Love Me
Too Many Parties & Too Many Pals	Mexicali Rose
Royal Telephone	I Love You More And More Everyday
One Road	Pearly Shells
Smile	Beautiful Woman
Eternally	Is This Love
Christmas In The Air	Down Below
Too Many Times	Under The Milky Way
Walking Talking Teardrop	The Way I Made You Feel
Wildflower	Thank You For The Dreamtime
Husbands And Wives	Surely God Is A Lover
There's A Heartache Following Me	You Put A Spell On Me
Anne	This Is The Truth

TREASURE: THE VERY BEST OF JIMMY LITTLE

2012	Warner Records	CD
Yorta Yorta Man	Surely God Is A Lover	
Under The Milky Way	Life's What You Make It	
Baby Blue	Stand By Me	
Mysteries Of Life	Resonate In Blue	
Shadow Of The Boomerang	Down The Road	
Beautiful Woman	Danny Boy	
Randwick Bells	Royal Telephone	
Winterwood		

SONGMAN (3 DISC SPECIAL)

2013	Warner Records	CD
Disc 1: Messenger	**Disc 2: Life's What You Make It**	
Down Below	Under The Bridge	
Under The Milky Way	People Get Ready	
The Way I Made You Feel	Look Out For My Love	
Randwick Bells	Life's What You Make It	
Quasimodo's Dream	One	
Into Temptation	What's So Funny About Peace Love & Understanding	
Cattle And Cane	One Line	
(Are You) The One That I've Been Waiting For	In My Room	
Blackfella Whitefella	My Father's House	
Alone With You	On Sacred Sands	
Bring Yourself Home To Me	Stand By Me	

SONGMAN (3 DISC SPECIAL CONT.)

2013   Warner Records   CD

Disc 3: Live At the Studio, Sydney Opera House

Under The Milky Way	Australia Downunder
Cattle And Cane	Into Temptation
Randwick Bells	Blackfella / Whitefella
Alone With You	Wide Open Road
Quasimodo's Dream	It's A Long Way To The Top
Can't Help Falling In Love With You	Almost With You
Royal Telephone	Family Man
Shadow Of The Boomerang	The Way I Made You Feel

AT LAST

2013   Opal Records   CD

I Don't Think She's In Love Anymore	I Will Love You All My Life
It'll Be Her Loving Me	Pass Me By
Maggie	And When I Dream
Ride Me Down Easy	Gene Autry Medley
Sweet Memories	Dusty Old Cowboy
Something That I Didn't Do	Royal Telephone
Trying To Outrun The Wind	Don Williams Medley

Duets

'Silver City Comet', Jimmy Little and Dick Carr & His Buckaroos, 1959, *Silver City Comet / The Grandest Show of All*, EMI Records

'Grandest Show Of All', Jimmy Little and Dick Carr & His Buckaroos, 1959, *Silver City Comet / The Grandest Show of All*, EMI Records

'Man Of Peace', Jimmy Little and Tania Worth, 1988, *The Ballad of Bobby White & Billy Black / Man of Peace*, Bunyip Records

'The Ballad Of Bobby White & Billy Black', Jimmy Little and Tania Worth, 1988, *The Ballad of Bobby White & Billy Black / Man of Peace*, Bunyip Records

'Holding You', Jimmy Little and Jean Stafford, 1995, *Yorta Yorta Man*, Monitor Records

'This Ancient Land', Jimmy Little and John Williamson, 2000, *John Williamson – The Platinum Collection*, Gumleaf Recordings

'Bury Me Deep In Love', Jimmy Little and Kylie Minogue, 2001, *Bury Me Deep in Love*, Festival Mushroom

'Happy Day', Jimmy Little and Olivia Newton-John, 2002, *2*, BMG

'Down The Road', Jimmy Little and Troy Cassar-Daley, 2003, *Down the Road*, ABC Records

'A Reason For It All', Jimmy Little and James Henry, 2003, *Down the Road*, ABC Records

'Reach Out', Jimmy Little and Melinda Schneider, 2003, *Down the Road*, ABC Records

'Baby Blue', Jimmy Little and Warren H. Williams, 2004, *Country Friends & Me*, CAAMA Music

'Blackfella / Whitefella', Jimmy Little and Ursula Yovich, 2008, *The Black Arm Band with the Melbourne Symphony Orchestra*, Arts House

'I Remember', Kate Ceberano and Jimmy Little, 2010, *Merry Christmas*, Universal Music Australia

Frances Peters-Little

Album appearances

'King of the Road', Jimmy Little, 1973, *The Stars of Australian Clubs*, Calendar Records

'Mysteries of Life', Jimmy Little, 1973, *Country Style Volume 1*, World Record Club

'Let's Meet Jimmy Little', The Wiggles and Jimmy Little, 2000, *It's a Wiggly Wiggly World*, ABC Music

'The Gods Will Lift You', Vika & Linda Bull, Jimmy Little and Deborah Conway, 2000, *Olympic Record*, WEA

'Resonate in Blue', Jimmy Little, 2001, *Festival Music Publishing / The 2001 Sampler Vol. 02*, Festival Records

'Into Temptation', Jimmy Little, 2001, *WOMAD In the Park: Sounds of WOMADelaide 2001*, WOMAD Records

'Royal Telephone', Jimmy Little, 2002, *Turn Up Your Radio – A Big Backyard Special*, The Big Backyard Label

'Baby Blue', Jimmy Little and Warren H. Williams, 2004, *Country Friends & Me*, CAAMA Music

'Thank You for the Dreamtime', Jimmy Little, 2005, *Brave New Day – An Australian Collection for Tsunami Aid*, Oxfam Label

'Cottonfields', Jimmy Little, 2005, *The Dig Australian Blues Project*, ABC Music

'Blackfella / Whitefella', Jimmy Little and Ursula Yovich, 2008, *The Black Arm Band with the Melbourne Symphony Orchestra*, Arts House

'I Remember', Kate Ceberano and Jimmy Little, 2010, *Merry Christmas*, Universal Music Australia

The EMI Sessions (1956-1958)

These tracks were recorded by EMI Records in Sydney between 1956 and 1958. The tracks are listed in the order of recording. Album compilation, remastering and track listing notes were compiled by Michael Alexandratos. All masters and transfers courtesy of country music collector David Crisp.
The full recordings can be accessed on YouTube via the QR code on page 243.

1. **THE HEARTBREAK WALTZ**
    Written by Jimmy Little and Pat Ware
    Recorded August 2, 1956
    Performed by Jimmy Little, with Pat Ware (guitar) & Alby Horton (bass)

2. **SOMEDAY YOU'RE GONNA CALL ME**
    Written by Jimmy Little and Pat Ware
    Recorded August 2, 1956
    Performed by Jimmy Little, with Pat Ware (guitar) & Alby Horton (bass)

3. **THE MYSTERIES OF LIFE**
    Written by Pappy Stewart
    Recorded August 2, 1956
    Performed by Jimmy Little, with Pat Ware (guitar) & Alby Horton (bass)

4. **STOLEN MOMENTS**
    Written by Joe Sherman and Sid Wayne
    Recorded August 2, 1956
    Performed by Jimmy Little, with Pat Ware (guitar) & Alby Horton (bass)

5. **SWEET MAMA**
   Written by Jimmy Little and Pat Ware
   Recorded November 13, 1956
   Performed by Jimmy Little, with Pat Ware (guitar) & Alby Horton (bass)

6. **A FOOL SUCH AS I**
   Written by Bill Trader
   Recorded November 13, 1956
   Performed by Jimmy Little, with Pat Ware (guitar) & Alby Horton (bass)

7. **IT'S TIME TO PAY**
   Written by Jimmy Little and Pat Ware
   Recorded November 13, 1956
   Performed by Jimmy Little, with Pat Ware (guitar) & Alby Horton (bass)

8. **MY FOOT IS ON THE STAIR**
   Written by Eric Watson and Jimmy Little
   Recorded November 13, 1956
   Performed by Jimmy Little, with Pat Ware (guitar) & Alby Horton (bass)

9. **THE GRANDEST SHOW OF ALL**
   Written by Jimmy Little and Pat Ware
   Recorded October 3, 1957
   Performed by Jimmy Little, with Dick Carr & His Buckaroos

10. **GOLDEN WRISTWATCH**
    Written by Wally Fowler
    Recorded October 3, 1957
    Performed by Jimmy Little, with Dick Carr & His Buckaroos

11. WHY MUST THERE BE A TOMORROW

Written by Eric Watson and Jimmy Little
Recorded October 3, 1957
Performed by Jimmy Little, with Dick Carr & His Buckaroos

12. THE SILVER CITY COMET

Written by Jimmy Little and Pat Ware
Recorded October 3, 1957
Performed by Jimmy Little, with Dick Carr & His Buckaroos

13. FRANCES CLAIRE

Written by Jimmy Little
Recorded May 7, 1958
Performed by Jimmy Little, with Dick Carr & His Buckaroos

14. WAITING FOR YOU

Written by Jimmy Little
Recorded May 7, 1958
Performed by Jimmy Little, with Dick Carr & His Buckaroos

15. THE COLOURED LAD

Written by Jimmy Little
Recorded May 7, 1958
Performed by Jimmy Little, with Dick Carr & His Buckaroos

16. OH! LONELY HEART

Written by Jerry Reed
Recorded May 7, 1958
Performed by Jimmy Little, with Dick Carr & His Buckaroos

The EMI Session recordings are available to listen via the QR code

Credits

The following have been reproduced with permission from their copyright holders. Listed by page number.

Front cover: Photography by John Elliott.

Back cover: Photography by Pierre Baroni. Gratefully reproduced with the permission of Pierre Baroni's estate.

10: Image of Sissy McGee: Author's own collection.

11: Image of the Wallaga Lake Gum Leaf Band: Courtesy of AIATSIS, Eileen Morgan Collection, item MORGAN.E02.BW-N05529_20.

52: Image of Jimmy at Nowra School of Arts Talent Quest: Author's own collection.

61: Image of Kunkus Little at Martin Place: Reproduced with permission from Nine/*The Sydney Morning Herald*. Photographer: Harry Martin.

66: Image of Jimmy Little and Pat Ware: Photo supplied by Tamworth Regional Council, operator of the Australian Country Music Hall of Fame.

86: Image of Jimmy and Marj Little: Photo produced with permission from Nine/*The Sydney Morning Herald*. Photographer: Noel Stubbs.

101: Image of Jimmy and Frances Peters-Little: Photo reproduced with permission from News Ltd./Newspix © News Ltd.

115: Image of the 'Royal Telephone' album artwork taken from Jimmy's personal scrapbook. Photography of the scrapbook by Juno Gemes.

132: Promotional poster for the *All Coloured Show* taken from Jimmy's personal scrapbook. Photography of the scrapbook by Juno Gemes.

137: The Jimmy Little Trio: Author's own collection.

165: Jimmy Little and John Blair on the set of *Black Cockatoos*: Author's own collection/taken from Jimmy's personal scrapbook. Photography of the scrapbook by Juno Gemes.

169: Promotional poster for the Brian Young Show taken from Jimmy's personal scrapbook. Photography of the scrapbook by Juno Gemes.

181: Picture of Jimmy at the launch of *Messenger*, courtesy of Sean Kennedy and Brendan Gallagher.

203: Picture of Jimmy holding his guitar © John Elliott, 2005.

Picture section:

Picture of Jimmy, Kunkus Little and Dora Williams: Author's own collection.

Shadow of the Boomerang film poster: Author's own collection/taken from Jimmy's personal scrapbook. Photography of the scrapbook by Juno Gemes.

Clippings from Jimmy's scrapbook: Author's own collection/taken from Jimmy's personal scrapbook. Photography of the scrapbook by Juno Gemes.

Jimmy being inducted into the ARIA Hall of Fame: Reproduced with permission from News Ltd./Newspix. Photographer: Jim Trifyllis.

Jimmy and Kylie Minogue: Reproduced with permission from David Anderson © 2001.

Jimmy performing with his brother and sisters: Author's own collection.

Jimmy and James Henry Little: Reproduced with permission from News Ltd./Newspix. Photographer: Jeff Darmanin.

Jimmy and Buzz Bidstrup: Courtesy of Buzz Bidstrup.

Jimmy and Buzz with the Purple Bus: Courtesy of the Jimmy Little Foundation.

Jimmy and Frances: 'Jimmy and Frances visit us on the Hawkesbury River' – Juno Gemes ©/ Juno Gemes Archive, 2010.

Image from Jimmy and Marj's wedding: Author's own collection.

The Little family celebrating Jimmy and Marj's 50th wedding anniversary: Author's own collection.

Jimmy's memorial concert: Reproduced with permission from Nine/*The Sydney Morning Herald*. Photographer: Peter Rae.

Walgett Water Tower mural: Reproduced with permission from Zest Events International.

Acknowledgements

For their support and for their wisdom, I would like to thank the following people for the role they played in getting this book to the end of its journey. Thank you to Professors Ann Curthoys and Peter Read for being there at the outset and for encouraging me to write this biography. Thank you for supporting me before and after my father passed away, and for your continued support when I made the decision to ultimately not write my father's story for my thesis. Secondly I would like to thank Juno Gemes, John Maynard and Larissa Behrendt who believed in me, and who told me that I would be the best person to write my father's biography.

A special mention and thank you to Brendan Gallagher and Graham Buzz Bidstrup for their contributions, for without them the final chapters would never have been written.

Thank you to Ilona Crabb for assisting with the interviews over many years and to Cyril and Hazel Green and Colin Hardy, who I interviewed over the phone when the pandemic prevented me from meeting and interviewing them in person.

I would also like to thank Shino Konishi, Rani Kerin and Jane Lydon for inspiring me to return to my father's biography after I stopped writing it, and to Carole Lander for coming on board and helping me to finally release it and find a publisher.

My thanks also go to filmmakers Sean Kennedy and Simeon Bryan for allowing me to access the footage of Jimmy singing 'Yorta Yorta Man' in their film *Gentle Journey* (2003). Many thanks to the individuals and organisations who have given permission to use images of Jimmy in this book. Thanks in particular to Wendy Maybury, Glennys and Maxine Briggs, and Reuben Ingalls from the Australian Institute of Aboriginal and Torres Strait Islander Studies for archival photographs; and to Juno Gemes Photography and to John Elliott.

I would also like to offer my gratitude to my cousin Deborah Cheetham for writing the foreword, and to Troy Cassar-Daley and his manager Roxanne Brown for generously providing a quote for the cover of the book.

And finally, but certainly not least, I would like to express my eternal gratitude to my literary agent Lyn Tranter from Australian Literary Management and to Pam Brewster and Elena Callcott, who believed in Jimmy Little, me, and the book.

Index

Page numbers in italics refer to illustrations

A
A Changing Race (1964 documentary) 149
'A Choice of Three' by Jimmy Little 95–7
'Abdul the Fire-Eater' 106
Aboriginal people
   Australia's assimilation policies 85, 87–8
   competing with immigrants for jobs and accommodation 90–1
   influence of Christianity 12
   native language and English usage 12
   relationships to land and family 16
   self-determination 152–3
   'urban tribes' 88–90
Aboriginal Protection Board (APB)
   establishing missions in Vic and NSW 19
   responses to the Cummeragunja strikes (1939) 22–3
Aboriginal Tent Embassy 153
Aboriginal Welfare Board 27, 214–45, 217–79
   an ever-present threat 45–7
   an instrument of assimilation 92
   arranges domestic work for Marj and her sisters 92–4

Aborigines Protection Acts 214–45, 218–91
Akers, Frank 107
All Coloured Show 91, 128–9, 131–6
Andrew, Auriel 78, 217–76
Anu, Christine
   on Jimmy 204
Arentz, Nelson 137
assimilation policy 85, 87–8
At Last album 185
Atkinson, William 24
Australian music scene
   late 50s and 60s 112–13
   television variety shows 122
Australia's Amateur Hour 67

B
'Baby Blue' by Jimmy Little 153
Baker, Glenn A. 183
Bandler, Faith 145
Bandstand television program 78
Barambah, Maroochy 167
Barham forest 30
Barton, Grace (nee McGee) (Jimmy's aunt) 24–5
Batley, Noelene 130
'Beautiful Woman' by Jimmy Little 157
Bennett, Kevin
   memories of Jimmy 204

Beulah, Lorna 129
Bidstrup, Graham 'Buzz' 179–80, 184, 192–3
   memories of Jimmy 204
Black Cockatoos play by Michelle Harrison 165
Black Mary film by Julie Janson 165–6
Black River film by Kevin Lucas 167
Black Theatre Company 152
'Black Tracker' by Jimmy Little 57–8
Blacksmith, Jimmie 56
Blair, Harold 144
Bomaderry Aboriginal Children's Home 46
Bond, John Alick 56
Boorooma station 105
Bowraville
   segregation at the picture theatre 145
Brewarrina Mission 105, 107
Brian Young country tours 168–9
Brierly, Bill (Jimmy's uncle) 54
Brierly, Jane 'Aunty Jane' (Jimmy's aunt) 38, 52
   cares for Jimmy and his siblings 45–6, 85, 87
Brierly, Walter 38
Brindle, Ken 145, 150
Briscoe, Gordon 145
   on the importance of Jimmy's work 149
Bryan, Simeon 186
Burton, Ray 131

C
Callaghan, Mark 183
Captain Thunderbolt 105, 166–7
Cassar-Daley, Troy 184
Ceberano, Kate 185
Cheetham, Deborah (Jimmy's niece) 60

Eumeralla, A War Requiem for Peace 60
   memories of Jimmy vii–xi, 204
Pecan Summer ix, x, 60, 204
'Chiller Trail' film by BP Australia 164
Clague, Joyce 145
Clark, Maggie 65
'coconut' (slang term) 143–4
Col Joye and the Joy Boys 121, 122
'Continental Duo' 69
Cooper, William 8, 22, 213–35
Cootamundra Domestic Training Home for Aboriginal Girls 46, 121
Countdown 157
Cummeragunja Choir 10, 13–14
Cummeragunja Mission 8–10, 15, 26
   Church of Christ 188–9
   corrupt management practices 21
   decline 31
   strikes (1939) 22–3
   treatment of 'agitators' 19, 212–20
   tuberculosis 21–2, 214–38
Cummeragunja Performers 11

D
'Danny Boy' sung by Jimmy Little 76
Danvers, J.G. 21
Dave Bridge Band 130
Davenport, Charles 106
Davis, Clayton 129
Davis, Oscar 110–12
Dawn Magazine 92
Dawson, Smoky 78
Day of Mourning (1938) 144
Denholm, Daniel 184
Devine, Candy 134
Dhungala (Murray River) 15
didgeridoo playing 14

Donaldson, Robert Thomas
218–91
treatment of Angledool's residents
105
Donovan, Casey
memories of Jimmy 204
Down The Road album 184
Dusty, Slim
importance to Jimmy 68

E
Eadie, Stuart 178
'El Paso' by Jimmy Little 76
Elliot, John
portrait of Jimmy 203, 209
Eora Centre 158–60, 163
Eumeralla, A War Requiem for Peace
by Deborah Cheetham 60

F
Fanning, Bernard 183
Federal Council for the Advancement
of Aborigines (FCAA) 144
Federal Council for the Advancement
of Aborigines and Torres Strait
Islanders (FCAATSI) 144–6
Fenech, Paul 167
Festival of Pacific Arts 170
Festival Records 110, 157, 179, 185
Jimmy's 'Christian songs' 117–19
Fisher, Bettie 129, 134
Flower, Dulcie 145
Foundation for Aboriginal Affairs
(FAA) 150
'Four Seasons of Life' by Jimmy Little
155–6
Frail, Fredia (Marj's aunt) 107
'Frances Claire' by Jimmy Little 73, 100
Fred Hollows Foundation 194
Freedom Ride 145–6

G
Galeazzi, Michael 178
Gallagher, Brendan 175–81, *181*, 183
memories of Jimmy 204
touring with Jimmy 181–2
Gallagher, Lee-Anne *181*
Galway, Ethel (nee McGee) (Jimmy's aunt) 24
Galway, William 24
Garma Festival 195
Geddes, Bill 150
Georgiadis, Costa *181*
Gingie Mission 105
'Give the Coloured Lad a Chance'
by Kunkus Little 59–60, 73, 221–124
Governor, Jimmy 56
Grand Ole Opry show 111–12
Green, Cyril 136, *137*
Groves, Bert 145
'Guided By His Love' by Jimmy Little 187–8
Guivarra, Faye Ann 134
gumleaf playing 13–14

H
Hailey, Marty 184
Haines, Frank 186
Hanson, Senator Pauline 176
Hardy, Colin 57, 78, 129, 134, 217–77
Harp family employ Marj and Lillian
as domestic servants 92–4
Higgs, Johanna (Jimmy's great-grandmother) 19
hillbilly music's influence on Jimmy's music 69
Hippai Peters 105
'Homeland' by Jimmy Little 17–18

I

Ingram, Frances (nee Green) 18–19
Ingram, Oswald 'Osley' 18–19
Ives, Burl 114–15

J

'Jackey Jackey' (slang term) 143
Jacobsen, Kevin 131
James, Adam
  memories of Jimmy 204
James, Thomas Shadrach 19
Jimmy Little Community Centre
  (Lilyfield) 209
Jimmy Little Foundation (JLF)
  194–6, 209
Jimmy Little Memorial Fund
  (Walgett) 209
Jimmy Little Street, Moncrieff
  (ACT) 209
Jimmy Little Trio 69, *137*
  early performances 73
  second formation 136
Jimmy Little's Gentle Journey film by
  Sean Kennedy 185–6
Johnson, Carole 170
Joye, Col 130, 219–106
  tours with Jimmy 121

K

Kalang showboat 71–2
Kelly, Paul 183
  on Jimmy 204
Kempsey
  segregation at the swimming pool
    145
Kennedy, Melinda *181*
Kennedy, Sean *181*
  Jimmy Little's Gentle Journey
    185–6
Kidney Health Australia 194
Kim, Max 136
Kinchela Boys Home 46

King, Martin Luther 143
Knox, Roger 57
Koma, Mary Ann 37
Koondrook 30
Koori Rugby League Knockout 90,
  153
Koori United football team 153
de Kroo, Leo 198
Kunkus (*see* Little, Jimmy Edward
  'Kunkus' senior)

L

La Prouse All Blacks 90
La Prouse communities 91
Lawrie, Bunna
  memories of Jimmy 204
Leaf Band 53–4
Lee, Lonnie 78, 102, 121, 130
Lehman, Frederick, M. 114
'Life is like a Lottery' by Jimmy Little
  63–5
Life's What You Make It album
  184–5
Lindsay, Reg 78
Little, Betty (Jimmy's sister) 60, 190
  All Coloured Show 133
  born 26
Little, 'Chudda' (Jimmy's aunt) 26
Little, Colin (Jimmy's brother) 28,
  29, 32, 33, 60
  All Coloured Show 133
  birth 33
Little, Eddie (Charles) 'Sutt' 26
Little, Eliza (formerly Brierly;
  nee Penrith) (Jimmy's
  grandmother) 37–8, 47, 51, 56
Little, Ernest 21
Little, Frances Claire (Jimmy's
  daughter) 62, *101*, 170–1,
  184
  birth 99–100
  'Frances Claire' by Jimmy 100

252

Little, Frances 'Sissy' (nee McGee)
(Jimmy's mother) 10, *10*
   birth 20–1
   and the Cummeragunja Choir 10
   death 44–5
   marries Kunkus 16
Little, Freddy (Jimmy's brother) 60
   All Coloured Show 132
   born 25
   performs with Jimmy 103
Little, Harold (Jimmy's cousin)
   taken from his parents 46–7
Little, Ian (Jimmy's cousin)
   taken from his parents 46
Little, Jack 'Pickelo' (Jimmy's uncle)
   26, 38
   death 54
Little, James Henry (Jimmy's
   grandson) 62, 171, 184, 185
   memories of Jimmy 204
   performs at Jimmy's Memorial
      Concert 137
Little, Jimmy *115, 132, 137, 169,*
   181, 203
   on Aboriginal activists 150–1
   Aboriginal of the Year Award
      (1989) 191
   All Coloured Show 132–6
   assimilation pressure 87–8
   auditions and talent quests 52,
      52–3, 67
   Aunty Jane 85, 87
   Bandstand 78
   birth 15
   charity work recognised 191
   Christian and Aboriginal spiritual
      beliefs 119–20, 188–90
   'Continental Duo' 69
   criticised for his success 141–2,
      148–9
   death 198–200
   deaths of siblings 21–2

   on domestic violence 190
   duets with well-known artists
      185
   early influences 68–9
   early sense of alienation 30–1
   employment discrimination 90–1
   Eora Centre 158–60
   expands musical horizons 76–7
   Festival Records 74
   film roles 75, 104, 117, 163–7
   Foundation for Aboriginal Affairs
      150
   full time artist 74–5
   Golden Guitar Award 197
   Goulburn home life 24–5
   health problems 172
   honorary doctorates 192
   on intolerance and cruelty 141–2
   Jimmy Little Foundation (JLF)
      194–6
   Jimmy Little Trio 69, 73, 136,
      137
   joins his father working 45, 51
   kidney failure, dialysis and
      transplant 192–4
   Kunkus and Jimmy perform
      together 62
   live theatre roles 165
   Living National Treasure (2004)
      192
   Marj and Jimmy marry 75, 83–5,
      97–9
   Marj's death 197–8
   memorial service 202
   Mo Award (1997) 191
   Monday Conference 149–50
   mother's death 44–5
   Nowra home life 25–6
   NSW Senior Australian of the
      Year (2002) 191
   Order of Australia Award (2004)
      192

253

Pat Ware collaborations 72–4
racial barriers 146–8
on racial equality in Australia 160–3
radio and its early importance 68
reception of 'Royal Telephone' 118–19
Red Ochre Award (2004) 191–2
Redfern in the 70s 152
Regal Zonophone 72–4
retires to Dubbo 196–7
'returns' to the stage 180–3
Riverina home life 26–32
'Royal Telephone' becomes a hit 78
school life at Terara 39–41
Shadow of the Boomerang (film role) 75–6, 104, 117, 163–4
Six O'Clock Rock 78
on Slim Dusty 68–9
solo work in the 1950s 71–2
support for Aboriginal performers 127–9
Sydney bound in 1953 65
Sydney's inner city 91–2
touring in the early 60s 129–30
2SM radio 77–8
on 'urban tribes' 88–9
US offer 110–12
Wallaga home life 51
Woorigee home life 37–47
Little, Jimmy (albums, songs and poems)
'A Choice of Three' 95–7
At Last album 185
'Baby Blue' 153
'Beautiful Woman' 157, 171
'Black Tracker' 57–8
'Danny Boy' 76
Down The Road album 184
'El Paso' 76
'Four Seasons of Life' 155–6
'Frances Claire' 73, 100
'Guided By His Love' 187–8
'Homeland' 17–18
'Life is like a Lottery' 63–5
Life's What You Make It album 184–5
Live At The Studio, Sydney Opera House 2001 album 185
Messenger album 175–81
'Money Matters' 125–7
Passage album 185
'Reincarnation' 173–4
Resonate album 183–4
'Round the Campfires of Old Wallaga Lake' 49–51
'Royal Telephone' 78, 109–10, 114, 116–17
Songman album 185
'The Coloured Lad' 59–60, 73, 221–124
The Definitive Collection album 185
'The Last Rose of Summer' 76
'This Lucky Old Sun' 76
Treasure: The Very Best of Jimmy Little album 185
'Waterloo Town Hall' 81–3
'Who's to Say' 139–40
'Woorigee' 35–7
'Yorta Yorta Man' 7–8
Little, Jimmy Edward 'Kunkus' senior 11, 37, 61
death 58–9
'Give the Coloured Lad a Chance' 59–60, 73, 221–124
in performance 13
'Queensland Song' 57
vaudeville background 9
Wallaga Lake Gum Leaf Band 9–13, 11, 53, 59
Little, John Edward (Jimmy's grandfather) 38, 62
kidnapping and early life 55
work as a tracker 56–7

Little, Lena (nee McGee) (Jimmy's aunt) 38
Little, Madeline Elizabeth 21
Little, Marjorie Rose 'Marj' (nee Peters) 86
  birth 104
  courts and marries Jimmy 75, 83–5, 97–9
  death 197
  employed as a domestic 92–4
  extended family 97–9
  family history 104–8
  health problems 172, 192, 196–7
  as Jimmy's business partner 102–3
  life and work in Sydney 85
Little, Monica (Jimmy's sister) 38, 60, 190
  All Coloured Show 133
  Deborah Cheetham 60
Little, Walter 'Bardi' 26
Little, William 'Darlo' 26
Live At The Studio, Sydney Opera House 2001 album 185

M

Martin, Jimmy 137
Mason, Dave 183
Maza, Bob 174
McCarthy, Malarndirri 193
McCracken, Jenny
  portrait of Jimmy 209
McGee, Bella (Jimmy's aunt) 23
McGee, Ernest (Jimmy's grandfather) 19–20
  death 32
  early life 20
McGee, Ernest Jnr 'Foxy' (Jimmy's uncle) 27
McGee, Frances 'Sissy' (*see* Little, Frances 'Sissy' (nee McGee) (Jimmy's mother))

McGee, George (Jimmy's great-grandfather) 19
McGee, Janet (nee Ingram) (Jimmy's grandmother) 19
  death 31
  marries Ernest McGee 20
McGee, Leslie (Jimmy's uncle) 24
McLeod, Arthur 61
McLeod, Bob
  on the importance of Jimmy's work 149
McMullen, Jeff
  memories of Jimmy 204
McQuiggan, A.J. 21–2, 32
Merritt, Robert 158–9
Messenger album 175–81
Minogue, Kylie 185
Moffatt, Tracey
  use of 'Royal Telephone' in *Night Cries* 119
'Money Matters' by Jimmy Little 125–7
Moonacullah Mission 19
Moree
  segregation at the swimming pool 145
Morgan, Chad 67
Morris, Shellie
  memories of Jimmy 204
Morton, Tex 68, 112
Mount Tulla Station 19
Murray, Neil
  memories of Jimmy 204
Murray River (Dhungala) 15
My Bush Book by Katie Langloh Parker 105

N

Namoi Reserve 105
National Aboriginal and Islander Skills Development Association (NAISDA) 170

Newton-John, Olivia 185
Night Cries by Tracey Moffatt 119
1967 Australian Aboriginals
    Referendum 146
NITV 194
Noffs, Rev Ted 150
Norman, Heidi
    on urban tribalism 90

O
O'Connor, Mark 184
O'Keefe, Johnny 122
On The Trail show (2SM) 102
Opals band 133

P
Page, Russell 167
Palmer, Don 194
Parsons, Jenny 60
Passage album 185
Patten, John (Jack) 22
Pecan Summer by Deborah
    Cheetham ix, x, 60, 204
Peckham, Ray 145
Penrith, Elizabeth 37
Perkins, Charles 145, 150
    on the importance of Jimmy's
    work 148–9
Peters, Benjamin (Marj's grandfather)
    105
Peters, Dahlia (nee Foster) (Marj's
    grandmother) 105
Peters, Doreen Claire (nee Simpson)
    (Marj's mother) 104, 105
Peters, Douglas (Marj's brother) 98,
    136, *137*
Peters, Elaine (Marj's sister) 98
Peters, Henry (Marj's father) 98,
    104–5
Peters, Lillian (Marj's sister) 98
    and the Harp family 92–4
Pleasance, Richard 184

Poitier, Sidney 143
Portrait of Australia film by Lloyd
    Shiels and Bede Whiteman 164
Purcell, Leah 183
Purple House 194–5
Purple Track 195

Q
Queenscliff Music Festival 180
'Queensland Song' by Kunkus Little
    57
Quigg, Ted 77, 102–4
    All Coloured Show 128–9
Quigley, Michael 178

R
Redfern
    changes in the 1970s 152
    communities 88, 91
Redfern All Blacks 90
Regal Zonophone 72–4
'Reincarnation' by Jimmy Little 173–4
Resonate album 183–4
Return to Country program 195
Riley, Emily (Marj's great-great-
    grandmother) 106
Riley, Tilly (Marj's great
    grandmother) 106
Roach, Archie 180
Rob E.G. 131
Robbins, Marty 76
Roseby Park 38–9
'Round the Campfires of Old
    Wallaga Lake' by Jimmy Little
    49–51
'Royal Telephone' by Jimmy Little
    78, 109–10
    composition 114
    reception and chart success
    116–17
    in Tracey Moffatt's *Night Cries*
    109–10

S

Schneider, Melinda 184–5
self-determination 152–3
Shadow of the Boomerang film 75, 104, 117, 163–4
Silva, Max 150
Silver Linings 150
Simms, Vic 121
Simpson, Archibald (aka Bilidju) (Marj's uncle) 98
    as 'Abdul the Fire-Eater' 106
Simpson, Clara 'Topsy' (nee Frail) (Marj's grandmother) 102, 105–6
    kidnap, rape and lost child 107
Simpson, George (Marj's uncle) 106
Simpson, Jack (Marj's uncle) 106
Simpson, Jack 'Smart Guy' (Marj's grandfather) 105–6
Simpson, John (Marj's great grandfather) 105
Simpson, Lulu (Marj's aunt) 106
Simpson, Maureen (Marj's cousin) 98
Six O'Clock Rock 78
Sole Brothers Circus 106
Somewhere into the Darkness film by Paul Fenech 167
Songman album 185
Stafford, Jean 185
Stanley, Jim 91
Stanley, Noel 91, 129, 134
Stewart, Rebecca (nee Little) (Jimmy's aunt) 47
Stone, Judy 120–1, 130
    memories of Jimmy 204
Stowe, Harriet Beecher 143
Sultan, Dan
    memories of Jimmy 204

T

Tamworth Country Music Festival 167–8
Tatura Internment Camps 26–7, 214–44
television
    impact on the music industry 78
    variety shows 122
Temby, David
    Down The Road review 184
Terara 38–41
Terara Public School 209
'The Coloured Lad' 59–60, 73, 221–124
The Definitive Collection album 185
'The Last Rose of Summer' by Jimmy Little 76
'This Lucky Old Sun' by Jimmy Little 76
Thorne, Nigel 136, *137*
Thumbs Up! program 195–6, 197, 209
Ti Tree School (NT)
    'Kumanjay Little' 200–1
Treasure: The Very Best of Jimmy Little album 185
Tredenick, Graham 'Nick' 69–70
tuberculosis at Cummeragunja 21–2, 214–38
Turner, Elizabeth 37
Turner, Thomas 37
2SM radio (St Mary's)
    On The Trail 77–8

U

Uncle Jimmy's Thumbs Up! program 195–6, 197, 209
Uncle Tom's Cabin by Harriet Beecher Stowe 143
United Aborigines Mission 46

Until the End of the World film by
    Wim Wenders 166
Uranquinty 33

V

Von Sydow, Max 166

W

Walgett 8, 104, 105, 218–92
    Jimmy Little Memorial Fund 209
    Jimmy Little portrait 209
    segregation at the picture theatre 145–6
Walker, Don 183
    memories of Jimmy 204
Wallaga Lake 9–10, 47–52
Wallaga Lake Aboriginal Reserve 51
Wallaga Lake Gum Leaf Band 9–13, 11, 53, 59
Ware, Pat 65
    background 67
    leaves the trio 74
    working with Jimmy 69–74
'Waterloo Town Hall' by Jimmy Little 81–3
Wave Hill strike 146

Wenders, Wim 166
'Who's to Say' by Jimmy Little 139–40
Williams, Buddy 68
Williams, Claude (Candy) 98, 129, 150
Williams, Dora 58
Williams, Margaret 61
Williams, Warren H. 185
    memories of Jimmy 204
Williamson, John 185
Woorigee 38–44
'Woorigee' by Jimmy Little 35–7
World War II 28–9
Wright, Frank
    portrait of Jimmy 209

Y

Yorta Yorta Country ix, 16, 33, 201
    Jimmy's final journey 199
    traditional lands 15, 33
'Yorta Yorta Man' by Jimmy Little 7–8
Yuin and Monaro clans 25
Yuin-Monaro Country 38
Yuwaalaraay people 105